THE CRICKETING FAMILY
EDRICH

BY THE SAME AUTHOR

Down in the Drink
The Ship-Busters
Strike Hard, Strike Sure
The Thousand Plan
Great Mysteries of the Air
Aviator Extraordinary
Verdict on a Lost Flyer
The Schneider Trophy Races
Against the Sea

The Last Blue Mountain
One Man's Jungle: a biography of F. Spencer Chapman

Ten Great Innings
Ten Great Bowlers
Test Cricket: England v. Australia
(with Irving Rosenwater)

THE CRICKETING FAMILY

EDRICH

Ralph Barker

with a statistical summary by
Irving Rosenwater

London
PELHAM BOOKS

First published in Great Britain by Pelham Books Ltd
52 Bedford Square, London WC1
1976

ISBN 0 7207 0909 1

Set and printed in Great Britain by
Tonbridge Printers Ltd, Peach Hall Works, Tonbridge, Kent
in Baskerville eleven on thirteen point on paper supplied by
P. F. Bingham Ltd, and bound by Redwood Burn
at Esher, Surrey

Contents

Acknowledgements

I should like to record my indebtedness to the Edrich family as a whole, and to Bill, Eric, Geoffrey, Brian and John in particular, for their enthusiastic and invaluable help in researching and compiling this account of their cricket careers.

Other members of the family who have helped considerably are W. A. Edrich and Edith Edrich, parents of Bill, Eric, Geoffrey and Brian (here for once the comment that 'there could have been no book without them' is literally true); G. H. Edrich (Uncle George); Mr and Mrs A. E. Edrich (Arthur and 'Midge'); and Rodney Edrich, who kindly gave me access to his unpublished history of the family origins.

Among those who helped most generously with comments and suggestions were Geoffrey Howard, Micky Stewart, Wilfred Wooller and the late Michael Falcon.

For an insight into the Norfolk scene I have relied principally on Bryan G. W. Stevens, of the *Eastern Daily Press* (himself a distinguished Norfolk county cricketer); and David J. M. Armstrong, the present county secretary.

A full list of my published sources is appended; but I must make special mention of *Runs in the Family*, by John Edrich as told to David Frith (Stanley Paul), and of various special articles that have appeared in *Wisden* and *The Cricketer* from which I have been given permission to quote. In a general way, too, these two publications have proved, as always, indispensable.

I must also acknowledge the help of the MCC Library and its Curator, Stephen Green; the Cricket Society and its Librarian, Peter Ellis; and the British Museum Newspaper Library at Colindale.

R.B.

Published Sources

Wisden Cricketers' Almanacks.

Norfolk County Cricket Club Annuals, Kent, Lancashire and Surrey County Cricket Club Year Books.

A Short History of Norfolk County Cricket, compiled by David J. M. Armstrong, (Ranchi House, Holt, Norfolk).

The Moon's A Balloon, by David Niven (Hamish Hamilton).

Official History of Lancashire County Cricket, by A. W. Ledbrooke (Phoenix House).

Lancashire, by John Kay (Arthur Barker).

Lancashire Hot-Pot, by T. C. F. Prittie (Hutchinson).

Runs in the Family, by John Edrich as told to David Frith (Stanley Paul).

Cricket Heritage, and *Cricketing Days*, by W. J. Edrich (both Stanley Paul).

Cricket Controversy, by Clif Cary (Werner Laurie).

Playing it Straight, by Ken Barrington (Stanley Paul).

The M.C.C. Tour of West Indies, 1968, by Brian Close (Stanley Paul).

Flying Bails, by Brian Statham (Stanley Paul).

Pace Like Fire, by Wesley Hall (Pelham Books).

Chucked Around, by Charlie Griffith (Pelham Books).

Assault on the Ashes, by Christopher Martin-Jenkins (Macdonald and Jane's).

Australia in England, 1964, by John Clarke (Stanley Paul).

The Geoffrey Edrich Benefit Book, 1955, edited by Eric Todd.

Basil Easterbrook, article on Norfolk and the Edrich Clan, *Wisden 1973,* in which he quotes Trevor Bailey.

John Reason, article in *The Cricketer Spring Annual* on John Edrich, April 1970.

Articles in *The Cricketer* by John Arlott, Colin Cowdrey, Jack Fingleton, Richard Streeton, and John Woodcock.

Various newspaper correspondents: notably the late L. N. Bailey of the *Star,* the late Sir Neville Cardus of the *Guardian*: Alf Clarke of the *Manchester Evening Chronicle*: John Kay of the *Manchester Evening News*: the late Denys Rowbotham of the *Guardian*: the late R. C. Robertson-Glasgow of the *Observer*: Peter Smith of the *News of the World*: E. W. Swanton of the *Daily Telegraph*: Eric Todd of the *Manchester Evening Chronicle*: E. M. Wellings of the London *Evening News*: Crawford White of the *Daily Express*: John Woodcock of *The Times*: and numerous unsigned contributions to the *Eastern Daily Press.*

Illustrations

9

Apart from the Edrich family, illustrations have been supplied by the following : Central Press, Sport and General, Press Association, Provincial Press, Eastern Daily Press, A. E. Coe and Sons, and E. & W. Fisk-Moore.

Prologue

The moment before the first ball is bowled in a new Test series
– as the batsman takes guard, the bowler limbers up, the field is
set and adjusted, and the umpire calls 'Play' – presents a scene
so charged with atmosphere and expectation that only, perhaps,
the emergence of the Cup Finalists from the tunnel at Wembley
can compare with it. When the protagonists are those oldest of
cricket adversaries, England and Australia, the tension becomes
almost palpable. Yet if it had been possible to measure, by
scientific instrument, the tension on the *second* day of the first
Test Match of 1975 at Edgbaston, all previous first-day read-
ings, if such had existed, would have been dramatically eclipsed.

All winter we had watched our finest batsmen facing an
intimidatory assault that had no parallel since the 'bodyline'
series more than 40 years earlier. One by one these batsmen,
almost without exception, had been found wanting. The names
of the men who had exploited their weakness had become house-
hold words. Lillee we knew, from a previous visit, as a great
fast bowler. Thomson was strange to us, except for the fearsome
glimpses we had seen of him on our television screens. Now we
were about to watch these two magnificent athletes in harness in
the flesh.

The batsman chosen to defy this opening onslaught was
thirty-eight years old. Only a year or so back it had been
assumed by many good judges that his international career
was over. No man's shortcomings at the crease were better
known. He was suspect outside the off stump. He was suspect
outside the leg stump. He couldn't – or he wouldn't – hook. And
he bore the scars of battle. Twice in the previous winter he had

paid for his errors, if errors they were, in broken bones. Yet of all the specialist batsmen who had been called upon to face that violent opening barrage, he was the only one whose reputation had not been torn to shreds. In the three Test Matches in which he had battled, often almost alone, against Thomson and Lillee he had averaged just under 40. Not until one looked down the order, to Tony Greig and Alan Knott, could one find anyone to compare with him.

It had been the resistance, as it happened, not merely of a man, but of a breed.

Confronting Lillee, then, as he bounded in towards the bowling crease from the pavilion end, was a short, sturdy figure with a name that had become synonymous with resolution and courage. It was the name of a tribe of yeoman farmers and cattle-dealers that had been known in Norfolk for centuries, a name that had its origins before the Norman Conquest. It was the name of Edrich.

This latest descendant of a family that had not, until the 1930s, claimed any particular distinction, had never let England down. He did not do so now. Indeed, in the course of the series he gained in stature, until, by the end of it, he took his place alongside Yorkshire's Maurice Leyland amongst left-handers as the greatest run-getter ever to confront Australia.

Forty years earlier, in 1935, the first great cricketing Edrich, W.J., had burst upon a sporting world from the comparative obscurity of a minor county by making a century against an international touring side. Yet this latest cricketing Edrich – and assuredly not the last – was first cousin to that earlier paladin. Their fathers, although brothers, were eldest and youngest of their generation respectively, fifteen years apart.

There had been other Edriches in first-class cricket in the intervening years, all full brothers to W.J. Geoffrey and Eric had played for Lancashire, Brian for Kent and Glamorgan. How was it that this long-established East Anglian family, threatened with extinction less than a hundred years earlier, should throw up, from the base camp of a single generation, five first-class cricketers, two of whom rose to the summit?

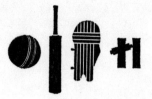

Mostly Bill

The name Edrich, although uncommon today, was by no means so rare in the Middle Ages, and it certainly predates William the Conqueror. Tracing a direct line is impossible, but it seems likely that the Norfolk Edriches took their name from the landholdings of Edric the Dane, which are recorded in the Domesday Book. There were certainly Edriches living in Norfolk in the fourteenth century; but the first Edrich we need to concern ourselves with is Harry Edrich, grandfather of Bill and John, born in 1868 and at that time precariously poised as the last of the line.

When little more than a child the young Harry Edrich contracted a poisoned arm which, through the application of a popular patent cure of those times, threatened not only his limb but his life. Fortunately, as it happened, the symptoms became so alarming that he was rushed to hospital, where both life and limb were miraculously saved. Those of us who have rejoiced in the cricket careers of the grandsons owe much to the skill and care of the doctors and nurses who restored the boy Harry to health and fitness a hundred years ago.

Still more do we owe, of course, to Harry himself. Marrying at the age of twenty-one, to a girl four years his senior, he wasted no time in starting a family. His first son, William Archer (Bill senior, father of E.H., W.J., G.A. and B.R.), was born in 1890, and almost annually for the next twelve years he and his wife Elizabeth increased their family. The future of the Norfolk Edriches was thus assured.

Long before this, however, the young Harry Edrich had begun another love affair – with cricket. Learning the rudiments of the game at Bracondale School, Norwich, where he was educated, he was playing regularly, by the time he was nineteen, for Burlingham Cricket Club, on the Burroughs estate near Blofield, about half-way between Norwich and Yarmouth, where his family were tenant farmers. This was in 1887. But since the game had been well established in Norfolk for more than a century, there is no certainty that he was the first of the Edriches to develop a passion for cricket.

Tradition has it that a cricket club existed at Swaffham as early as 1700; and by 1788, and probably many years before that, there was a club in Norwich. The standard at this time was probably low, however, as nine years later, in 1797, thirty-three men of Norfolk played Eleven of England and lost by an innings. But in January 1827 the Norfolk County Cricket Club was established, with a ground at Lakenham, Norwich, 'laid down with fine turf by Mr Bentley from Lord's', and such was the enthusiasm for the game in Norfolk by this time that they could not wait for the summer to start, a match being played in February on the frozen surface of the mere at Diss. Play began at ten o'clock in the morning and lasted until dusk, and 1,500 spectators watched the fun. Ladies' matches, too, were not uncommon, and the idea of a family match, later developed into a habit by the Edriches, first found favour at about this time, when six men named Alexander and five named Cushion played Litcham for two pounds a head and won by one wicket. Twenty-one years later, in 1846, eleven brothers Colman, of the mustard family, had the better of a draw in a two innings match against eleven resident members of the Norwich club.

Those intervening twenty-one years saw the emergence of Norfolk's most famous cricketer, a title not even the Edriches would dispute. Fuller Pilch, too, was a member of a prolific local family, whose descendants still play for Norfolk. Standing over six feet tall, he was the first great stylist of the game. But although in the early 1830s Norfolk was spoken of as 'the next club to Marylebone', and Pilch was keeping a public house and pleasure gardens on Bracondale Hill and seemed contented, like many a Norfolk-born cricketer after him he was tempted away from the county by inducements outside it, and from 1836 to 1854 he played mostly for Kent. For a time interest in the game in Norfolk fluctuated, and one critic, writing in 1842, noted that 'about two years since nothing appeared more probable than its extinction'. A revival was imminent, however, and in 1844 Norfolk beat the MCC for the first time for many years, and five years later they beat an All-England XI at Norwich. When the young Harry Edrich began to play for Burlingham twenty-five years later, the game had taken root in the fertile Norfolk soil.

After his marriage to a Norfolk girl named Elizabeth Barcham in 1889, Harry Edrich farmed the Coxhill Farm at North Burlingham, and it was there, in the space of the next ten years, that his wife bore him eight children – five boys and three girls. In 1900 he moved to Church Farm, Lingwood, which boasted a quaint little farmhouse not far from the church, and was still on the Burroughs estate; but the move did not interrupt Elizabeth's annual child-bearing, as she gave birth to a sixth son in 1900, a seventh in 1901, and an eighth on Christmas Eve 1902, making eleven children in just over twelve years. In those days it was still possible for tenant farmers to afford to keep resident maids, and Elizabeth was provided with adequate help. Fears for her general health, too, seem to be misplaced, as when the breakdown came it befell not Elizabeth but Harry; in 1903, at the age of 45, trying to get back to normal too soon after double pneumonia and pleurisy, he was stricken with what was almost certainly poliomyelitis and from that time on was paralysed from the hips down. By this time, however, his reputation as a local cricketer was secure. 'As a bowler he was held in awe by batsmen of the period,' says a contemporary account, 'and as a batsman he could slog as occasion arose.' His incapacity did not for one moment abate his passion for the game. And fortuitously enough, although the annual achievement of paternity was interrupted, it did not stop altogether. A ninth son, Frederick Hugh, was born in 1905, and a fourth daughter,

Alice Miriam, in 1907, making thirteen children in all. Alice, known to the family as 'Cis', inherited or absorbed her father's involvement with cricket just as the boys did, and she was so good at it that she was later to captain the Norfolk ladies' team. Fred, the youngest son, was to have two children when the time came, a boy and a girl; the boy, John Hugh, was to become J.H. of Surrey and England.

What manner of man was this Harry Edrich? How was it that he begat this remarkable progeny? Knowing that he was the last of the line, he obviously considered it his duty to raise a large family. But his claims to recognition go far beyond mere fertility. Much of what was subsequently achieved by his sons and grandsons must be credited to his enthusiasm and influence. His personality, it seems, was charismatic, overcoming many of the frustrations and pitfalls which presented themselves in the East Norfolk of those days, where cricket was nothing like so firmly embedded in the public consciousness as it was in the south and west. A pacy bowler in his day, and a strong hitter, the carry of some of whose shots is still talked about locally, he started a club at Lingwood when he left Burlingham; and although the game in these Norfolk villages might not approach the standard of the organised club and league cricket of to-day, Harry Edrich's devotion to it survived not only crippling illness but also the blank years of the First World War and the depression that followed it.

Harry had always been determined to provide his children with an adequate education, and they were all sent either to Norwich or to Yarmouth to school. Bill senior, Edwin, Arthur, Charles and George, the five eldest boys, followed their father to Bracondale. Robert, Harry and John went to the Priory School in Great Yarmouth. The youngest boy, Fred, went to Norwich High School, and all four girls went to Wakefield House, Norwich. But it was the boys who went to Bracondale who got the best grounding in the subject most dear to them all.

Before his illness it was Harry's custom to drive himself round Norfolk in a pony and trap, partly to collect rents from his various properties, but principally to buy and sell livestock, of which he was the shrewdest of judges. Even after his illness he did not change his habits, merely sitting in his trap while the cattle were rotated in front of him. 'He'd go out during the week to buy bullocks,' recalls his son George, 'and then on the Friday night the men would collect them and walk them into Norwich. At the Saturday market he'd sit there on the Castle steps by the urinal and sell to the big dealers. When he'd sold out he'd drop down to the Cock Inn at the bottom of the market for a few double whiskies and a salt beef sandwich. Then he'd drive home. Sometimes, when he got out beyond Thorpe Griffin, about six miles from Lingwood, he'd drop off and let go of the reins, but the pony would take him home, trotting right into the yard.'

It was on the return trip from one of these forays that he fell foul of the law for having no lights. The policeman who stopped him was the local Bobby, a man named George Pile. 'I'll have to charge you, Mr Edrich,' says Pile. 'You won't do that, George?' 'Yes, I will,' says Pile; and he was as good as his word. The chairman of the magistrates who heard the case was a farmer named Wyllie, for whom Harry Edrich had often bought bullocks. 'You're fined £2,' said Wyllie severely. 'Very good, sir,' said Edrich. But under his breath he added: 'All right, old boy. I'll put another half-a-crown apiece on your bullocks.' And in due course he got his £2 back, with interest.

The handicap of partial paralysis, however, inevitably had its repercussions on the farm. Another pair of hands became mandatory, not necessarily skilled, and at the end of the summer term of 1904, when he was not quite fourteen, Bill Edrich senior's days at Bracondale School were cut short. He had been a good student, judging from the letter the Headmaster's wife wrote, at the end of that term, to Mrs Harry Edrich.

Dr. Wheeler and I were both very sorry to hear from Mr Edrich that Willie was to leave at mid-summer.

He had been doing so well and working so hard at his lessons, that it does seem a pity that he should leave just when he is taking such an interest in his education, and when a little longer at school would be of such benefit to him.

He is a very nice boy and no one could work better so that we shall be very sorry to part with him.

It is a comfort however to feel that he is so reliable, and I can quite understand that his father in his delicate state of health feels he wants him at home.

It is unlikely that the boy suffered much from the change. Already literate, and good at figures, he learned as quickly on the farm as at school. His cricket probably suffered at first, but Harry Edrich was not one to deny his sons any chance of a game, and Bill played regularly for Lingwood for the next ten years. In fact he developed into a sound wicket-keeper batsman who generally opened the innings, in a side that often boasted four Edrich brothers in its ranks. In his work he was well on the way to becoming one of the best tenant farmers in Norfolk in his own right. And in 1913 he got married, to a pretty, warm-hearted Cumberland girl named Edith Mattocks, whose parents had exchanged their Cumbrian acreage for the more productive land of East Anglia. Four months before the outbreak of war, on 27th March 1914, she gave birth to a son, Eric Harry, who was to inherit her bright, gently ebullient nature. From his father he would take his good-natured strength, his small stature, and his skill, when the time came, as a wicket-keeper batsman.

With the outbreak of war, and the exacerbations of the U-Boat campaign, farming in all its aspects took on a special significance; but eventually Bill was called upon to report for medical examination. To his dismay he failed it, and next morning he went to the family doctor to find out what was wrong. Nothing, said the doctor. The recruiting authorities in Norwich knew Harry Edrich, and knew too of his disability; this was their way of ensuring continuity on the farm. Thus Bill was spared the holocaust which ended or ruined the lives of so many of his contemporaries. He was free to return to the work he loved, and to the task of raising a family. On 26th March 1916, two years all but a day since the arrival of Eric,

Edith gave birth to a second son, William John. And before the war ended, on 13th July 1918, a third son, Geoffrey Arthur, arrived.

When the armistice was signed in November 1918, there were nearly six months available in which to prepare for the 1919 season; and despite the four dreadful years of carnage, the first-class counties somehow managed to renew their old antagonism, albeit on a two-day basis. The minor counties, however, delayed the resumption of their competition until 1920, confining themselves to informal friendlies in 1919. It was in one of these friendlies that an Edrich first played for Norfolk.

The Edrich brothers were well known in Norfolk club cricket by this time, particularly Bill as a wicket-keeper batsman, Edwin as a pacy bowler and attacking batsman very reminiscent of his father, and George as a batsman. Bill was now twenty-nine and Edwin twenty-eight, and both were invited to play for Norfolk Club and Ground. Later in that 1919 season the two men were present at the county ground at Lakenham to watch Norfolk play a two-day match against A Cambridge XI, as the undergraduates' team was designated. It was roughly of Cambridge Crusaders strength and included several men who had played in the early-season trial matches. Norfolk fielded a side composed mostly of county players. Shortly before the start, Bill was approached by Gibson, the Norfolk professional bowler. 'Can you play?' asked Gibson, 'we're one short.' 'I haven't got my things here,' replied Bill. Gibson turned to Edwin. 'Can *you* play?' 'I'll play if you can find me some gear.' This of course was the answer Bill should have given; the distinction of being the first Edrich to represent his county thus fell to the younger of the two brothers.

The Cambridge XI batted first and made 129; although seven bowlers were called upon, Edwin was not among them. Norfolk collapsed after a steady start, but the tail wagged and they reached a total of 143, a lead on first innings of 14. Edwin, batting No. 8, contributed a useful 15 to the revival before he was run out. Cambridge at the second attempt made 154, and again the bowlers did not include Edwin. But his batting had evidently impressed the Norfolk captain, who put him in No. 3 in the second innings. After the fall of an early wicket, and equipped now with his own gear, Edwin batted with such authority that he made 71 out of Norfolk's winning total of 142 for two and was undefeated at the end.

This innings, so far above the achievement of anyone else in the match, marked Edwin as a batsman well up to minor counties' standard. Yet curiously enough he was never asked to play for Norfolk again. Nor indeed were any of the Edrich brothers. And it was not that their ability, or for that matter their natural charm of manner, were not well known. 'I played a lot of games for Norfolk Club and Ground in later years under R. G. Pilch,' recalls Bill senior. (Pilch was a grandson of Fuller and the grandfather of D.G., until recently the Norfolk captain.) 'I kept wicket, and I went in first. But I never got a chance for the county.' One of the reasons, undoubtedly, was that most of the matches were played in the summer vacation, and young men from the colleges and universities were given preference. Otherwise the fame of the cricketing Edriches, in that first post-war decade, would not have been confined to Norfolk.

It was to be left to the next generation of Edriches to spread the name far and wide. And by about this time, the first two of this generation, Eric and Bill, were beginning to show their paces on the lawn at Lingwood. Eric, naturally, was the first to face up to his father's lob bowling, but Bill could not be kept out of it. 'My first memory of taking even the smallest part in any game of cricket,' remembers Bill, 'was when I was three and Eric was five. My father had bought Eric a miniature bat, and he was bouncing a ball to him one evening while I was allowed to run after it and throw it back. My younger brother Geoffrey was already tucked up in his cot, and far too soon it got towards my own bed-time. We had a nursemaid in those days, but I didn't want to go, and when she picked me up I kicked and screamed.' Fifty years later he was to go on record as saying that he would never give up cricket : cricket would have to give

22

him up. Metaphorically speaking, as in his childhood at Lingwood, he would rather be carried kicking and screaming from the scene.

In 1921 the Burroughs estate, of which the farm at Lingwood was a small part (170 acres), was sold, and although all the tenant farmers were expecting to be offered a portion, the Norfolk County Council bought the estate up for small holdings for men returning from the war, and the Edriches had to go. Harry Edrich bought Manor Farm, Blofield, where he lived until he died. Bill senior hired a farm at Cantley Manor, in the same part of Norfolk, and it was there, on 22nd August 1922, that a fourth son, Brian Robert, was born. A daughter, Ena, was born in 1924.

As soon as Brian was old enough, he joined his three brothers in cricket practice on an asphalt path leading up to the kitchen door, with a wicket marked out on the door in chalk. 'That,' says Brian, 'is where Dad made me a left-hander. He put the bat in my hands and said : this is how you stand.' I said : 'What about the others?' He smiled and said : '*You* stand this way.' Brian was naturally right-handed, he bowled right-handed, and his left hand in fact was weak. Did Bill senior make Brian into a left-hander partly for the sake of variation, or because he wanted a left-hander in the family? Today he chuckles at the thought; but his memory on the point is clear. At an early age Brian picked up the bat one evening and shaped up left-handed, and his father, knowing the value of having the stronger hand gripping the top of the handle, did not interfere. When he noticed that the boy seemed to strike the ball rather better left-handed than right, he encouraged what seemed to him to be the boy's natural aptitude.

Each of the three older boys, when he was old enough, started his education at the local village school. And it was during these years at Cantley, with the chalked wicket on the kitchen door behind them, that the boys learnt the rudiments of batting. Using a proper cricket ball, but standing more or less still and turning their arms over from a distance of fifteen yards, Bill senior and his brothers bowled to the boys for hours

23

on end. 'It was a damned hard job to get one through,' remembers Uncle George. But that they tried, and sometimes
succeeded, is proved by the regular repairs that became necessary to the door.

One bowler who often got the ball past them was the
youngest of Harry Edrich's children, Alice Miriam. Not yet out
of her teens, she seemed to the boys to bowl as well as anyone,
and Uncle George agrees. 'She'd always been ready to make up
a team when we were young,' he says. 'She bowled pretty sharp,
and she hit the ball hard, and she learned the game just the
same as we did.'

But day in day out it was Bill senior who did the bowling.
'Play straight,' he would say, 'and keep over the ball when you
play the cut.' Although the boys were hitting into the farmyard
and away from the house, they all displayed such a partiality
for the cut that any windows within reach had to be covered
with wire netting. Bill senior, fond of the cut himself, never
tried to stop them. Meanwhile, in holiday times, they were
joined for more ambitious practice by their schoolfellows from
the village. These were better years for the farming community,
and at Christmas each of the boys could count on a beautiful
new bat of exactly the right size as a present, and a football
between the three of them.

It was during the summer holidays, though, that they enjoyed
the greatest treat of all – the annual August Bank Holiday visit
to Lakenham to see Norfolk play Hertfordshire. They had
watched their father and their uncles play in village cricket
often enough, but these county players, with their faultless
flannels and sweaters and their brightly-coloured caps, were
surely the top-notchers. You might read in the papers about
Surrey and Yorkshire, or the Australians, but there could be no
better cricket anywhere than this. 'I once saw the great Michael
Falcon, the man who bowled out the Australians in 1921 for
Archie MacLaren's team, take seven for 36,' remembers Eric
in his lilting Norfolk brogue. 'But the day I remember best was
in 1926, when C. H. Titchmarsh of Hertfordshire made 218.
He was only a little fellow, and he was hooking Michael Falcon

off his eyebrows. First he hit him to square leg, and when they moved fine-leg round he started hitting him fine. When he got to his 200 we were all cheering madly when a pigeon landed on the wicket, and Titchmarsh somehow got it to hop on to his bat. He held it up to the crowd to acknowledge the cheering, then sent it flapping off with a flick of the wrist. I thought the cheering would never stop.'

In that same year Eric, then twelve, and Bill, ten, went to Bracondale, and there they came under the watchful and benevolent eye of a man whom they both describe as the greatest of coaches. Jack Nichols was a cheery soul who had been on the playing staff of both Lancashire and Worcestershire before moving to Staffordshire, for whom he enjoyed considerable success as an all-rounder in the years preceding the war. Soon after the war Michael Falcon discovered him coaching at Bishop's Stortford College. 'This,' Falcon decided, 'is the man we want for Norfolk,' and Nichols was duly poached, playing for the county for the next ten years and remaining as coach until just before the Second World War. He had the gift, above all, of recognising what there was to work on in an individual pupil and bringing it out.

One of his tenets was that you couldn't teach a boy to play straight, head over the ball, unless the practice surface was reliable. Because of the heavy wear and tear on practice pitches he insisted on a matting surface laid on concrete, and when teaching boys the technique of playing forward he would butt them with his head. After coaching in the county nets at the beginning of the season he toured the principal schools in the Norwich district and thus came one day to Bracondale. With the co-operation of the sports master, F. E. Scott, a concrete wicket was provided.

Bill has related in one of his books how a square hit on the leg side, properly executed, would land the ball amongst the Headmaster's gooseberry bushes. 'Bowl us a gooseberry, Jack,' they would plead, when the Head was out of the way. With a sly look Jack Nichols would tempt the boys with deliveries that looked inviting but weren't always quite what they seemed, leaving them guiltily cross-batted as the bails fell. But the Edrich boys, as fond of gooseberries as any, soon learned to pick the right ball. Bill's proclivity for the hook, which some would call the pull, since it mostly went square or to mid-wicket, was developed, he believes, by this circumstance, which he was never tired of relating. Many a time, in the years to come, his most famous partner was to signal the execution of yet another Edrich hook with a whispered: 'That was a *gooseberry!*'

In due time Eric and Bill both got their colours at Bracondale, where school matches were played on the county ground at Lakenham, though not on the main square, which was roped off. Thus the fielders had to run right round the ropes to chase any ball hit hard enough on that side. Here was another invitation to perfect the 'gooseberry', which might bring a bonus of five or six all run.

The boys had hardly gone to Bracondale, however, when another family move became necessary, for the same reason as before; the farm at Cantley was sold over their heads. This time Bill senior hired another 500-acre farm at Upton. Curiously enough it offered a similar facility to the one that had been so popular at Cantley – a concrete path leading up to the kitchen door. And although rain could interfere with play, it could not stop it, since there was an alternative concrete wicket in the barn. While the bounce on these wickets was fairly reliable, the surface was minutely cratered and the ball would deviate, teaching the boys from the start to watch for movement off the pitch. With Bill senior sometimes taking the gloves behind them, eager for the snick, they learned the art of watching the ball right on to the bat, and of leaving the ball they didn't have to play.

Wherever Bill senior went he improved the land he worked on, and for the first few years at Upton he broke even; but by the time Geoffrey was ready to join his brothers at Bracondale, the first ripples of the depression years were spreading to Norfolk and farming was becoming an ever more precarious existence. Some sacrifice, it was clear, would have to be made. Bill, like his father, had proved a good student, and he was being groomed for the teaching profession, but Eric had no pretensions to being an academic and was looking to farming as a career. Thus in 1929, when he was fifteen, Eric's schooling was terminated and he joined his father at Hall Farm.

This was certainly no hardship for Eric. He loved the open-air life on the farm, and he began to get more cricket than he had ever had in his life. He played with his father for Upton, a club which, like Lingwood, the family had formed, he played with him for Blofield, and with Uncle George captaining East Norfolk, he frequently got a game for them. 'Being on a farm,' he recalls, 'I was always available.' Someone, generally Uncle George, would phone to ask his father: 'What about a game of cricket today?' The answer would often be: 'I'll try, but if I can't play, Eric will go,' or 'Sorry, we're working flat out here – but Eric will come.' Rather than inhibiting him in any way, his father always encouraged him to play. 'What about the farm work?' Eric would sometimes ask. 'That'll still be there tomorrow,' was the reply. 'It was marvellous,' says Eric, 'especially when Uncle George drove over to pick me up to play for East Norfolk. Uncle George was a great player to bat with, with a tremendous straight drive, and once, two or three years after I left school, I remember we were having a great race for our tons when I got out for 97. He got 108 not out. If he hadn't been such a successful cattle auctioneer he could have gone places in cricket.'

Meanwhile Bill, although progressing with his studies, was having even greater success with his cricket. In 1929, at the age of thirteen, he got his school colours as the baby of the team and played in the great blood match against Norwich High School at Lakenham, though with no great distinction. But in the ensuing year he began to fill out, and in the same match in 1930, bowling at an astonishing speed for a boy of his age, he took all ten Norwich High School wickets in 49 balls for 18 runs, all clean bowled. Despite his tender age he was made captain, and against Diss Secondary School that same year he scored his first century, 121 out of 168 for six declared, then took eight for 20 and caught another.

Surprisingly, he had not yet formed any clear-cut ambition to play first-class cricket, but the notion was there, and on Sunday afternoon walks with an adventurous boy named Geoff Pymer who wanted to be a speedway rider (and later became one), he confessed his dream. 'I want to be a professional cricketer and footballer.'

In 1931, still one of the smallest boys in the school XI, he dwarfed all others in ability, as shown by his 149 not out against City of Norwich School, made in an hour and three-quarters and including two sixes and 22 fours. Second top score, by the last man in, was 5 not out. 'I wish you'd come down here and have a look,' Jack Nichols told Michael Falcon, 'I think I've got a good one.' Falcon did so and was suitably impressed; but he resisted Nichols' pleas to put the boy straight in the County XI. A bad match at that age might destroy his confidence. But he was picked for the Norfolk Colts' match that August and made 57 out of 110 in two hours – by far his most mature innings yet – then took four wickets for one run in four overs before being taken off to give the other colts a chance.

Earlier that summer, another Edrich had represented Norfolk; this was Alice Miriam, or 'Cis', destined to captain the Norfolk ladies' team. The fame of the Edriches, although still confined to the county, was spreading, and on Wednesday 15th July of that year, at Blofield, an event took place which was often to be repeated in later years and which transcended the bounds of parochial news when the family turned out in strength to play East Norfolk. This by general consent was the first Edrich family match. 'They cannot equal the record of the Colman brothers,' wrote a correspondent, 'but we are informed the team will include eight brothers and three sons, and two other members of the family will officiate as umpire and scorer respectively.' Cis, described in the report as 'one of the best lady cricketers in the county', was the scorer; but she had an added interest in that her future husband was playing for East Norfolk. Unfortunately the weather was unkind and the match had to be abandoned after East Norfolk had reached 104 for four.

*　　*　　*

Early in the 1932 season Bill was one of five members of the Edrich family to turn out for Blofield in a league match against Norwich Wanderers, and out of Blofield's total of 162 he made 77. In the same match Edwin scored 45 and took five Wanderers' wickets for 11. 'We recall the days,' said one newspaper, 'when Blofield took a prominent part in the Senior Cup Competition, and the Edrich family have sufficient cricketing ability among them to raise the standard of Blofield cricket to at least its old level.' Thus surely comes into the realm of classics of understatement.

A performance like this in senior club cricket convinced Michael Falcon and others that the boy was ready for the county side, and when the first match of the season came, against All India on Thursday and Friday, 2nd and 3rd June at Lakenham, they threw their young sixteen-year-old in at the deep end. This was by far the strongest touring party ever to come from India up to that time. They played one Test Match, which but for two fighting innings by Douglas Jardine they would probably have won, and they won more than they lost of their twenty-six first-class matches. Moreover they had in Mohammed Nissar and Amar Singh two bowlers of international class. Amar Singh stood down against Norfolk, but Nissar, who was the cause of an early collapse three weeks later in the Test Match, was included as the spearhead. Tall and very big-boned for an Indian, with a nice easy action, he was probably the fastest bowler ever to represent the sub-continent, and when his pace was allied to a wicket which gave the bowlers some help, as on this day at Lakenham, he was a formidable figure indeed.

But first, Norfolk's own quicker bowlers took full advantage of the conditions to topple the Indians for 101. The young prodigy was given a chance with the ball, and in eight overs, three of which were maidens, he took the wicket of S. Nazir Ali, one of the tourists' leading batsmen, for 11 runs. The record shows that Nazir Ali was lbw, and that Jack Nichols was one of the umpires; but according to Bill he was standing at square leg.

Within a very short time the Norfolk innings had become a

29

procession, and when Bill came in at No. 7, five wickets were down for scarcely 20 runs. 'He was just a boy,' remembers Edith Edrich, who was watching in some trepidation with her husband, 'and the big dark Nissar was bowling. I almost fainted when I saw him walk out of the pavilion, he looked so small.' The whole of Bracondale school had been given a half-holiday for the event, and they roared their encouragement as their champion marched to the crease. What did it look like to a sixteen-year-old? 'I remember hanging on to my bat like grim death as Nissar approached with his long bounding run,' he has written, 'and the ball came from his hand and struck like lightning off the pitch.' There was a deafening cheer from the school, but he was simultaneously aware that he had missed the ball completely. It was in the wicket-keeper's hands. Blue turbans bobbed around him, and the keen dark countenances moved closer. 'As for me, I set my teeth so hard that they hurt, and my brain kept repeating that I must not get out without scoring.' That was the height of his ambition – to avoid the duck that would disgrace the school. Mohammed Nissar finished with figures of six for 14, and Norfolk were all out for 49; but by that time the boy Edrich was a hero. No one else had got into double figures, and before he became yet another of Nissar's victims Bill had made 20.

India then made 204 for nine declared, Edrich 0 for 28, leaving Norfolk 257 to win. They managed barely half that number, and only four men reached double figures; but Bill, with 16, was one of them. Of the Norfolk batting *Wisden* had only one comment. 'Edrich, a schoolboy, batted in promising fashion.'

Norfolk also had their eye on another promising Edrich in Eric, who was now eighteen and scoring consistently for Blofield. But when he was given his chance in a Club and Ground game he got a duck.

For the rest of that summer term it was back to school for Bill, and he missed the next three Norfolk matches. But he got two hundreds in July, one for the Club and Ground and one for Bracondale in a school match, and at the end of that month he was chosen to play against Leicestershire II at Leicester. Clean bowled in both innings without scoring, he collected his first 'pair' and was down to earth with a bump; but Michael Falcon kept faith in him through the lean spell that followed, and in the penultimate match of the season, against Buckinghamshire, who were champions that year, he top-scored in both innings with 50 – his first for Norfolk – and 23. In twelve innings that season he scored 181 runs for an average of 15.

Captain of football as well as of cricket at Bracondale, Bill wangled himself a few games with Norwich City Reserves – to use his own expression – that autumn, and his speed and zest were noted. But overshadowing all else at that time were his father's business worries. Crops were fetching less than they cost to grow, the livestock market was similarly depressed, and it had become impossible to make a living. Hall Farm had to be given up, and the outlook was bleak.

Then, in April 1933, a chance came to take over a Crown Lands farm in the Pocklington area, on the Yorkshire wolds. In that uncertain economic climate it had become impossible to let it, and the agents had decided to put a manager in to save the farm from deteriorating. They liked what they saw and heard of Bill Edrich senior and they gave him the job. But the salary was modest, and it looked like the end of Bracondale School for Bill and Geoffrey. Geoffrey had gained his school colours in 1932 and he was not yet fifteen, but now his education, and all that it meant to his development, was cut short. Bill, however, beginning to think seriously now about county cricket, was still being trained for the profession of schoolmaster, and thanks to the generosity of the Headmaster, who took him in as a boarder, he stayed for a further year. It is not perhaps cynical to suggest that his success at cricket must have been the best possible advertisement for the school, and certainly this must have occurred to Geoffrey. It was the first of many hard knocks that Bill's younger brother was to have to take from life, but fortunately he shared the Edrich resilience and moved happily to Yorkshire to work on the farm.

Nothing could have been more auspicious than the arrival of

the Edriches at Woodhouse Grange Farm, near Sutton-on-Derwent. They had hardly started unloading when a neighbouring cattle dealer invited them to stay the night at his farm. Yorkshire folk took to the Edriches, as they would take to them in later years, and the Edriches responded. These early friendships were soon cemented when their cricket ability became better known.

While Eric and his father played in senior cricket for Londesborough Park, Geoffrey, still only 15, played for the village of Elvington, three miles away. Both boys still benefited a good deal from the liberal attitude of their father when it came to a day off for cricket. 'We used to play a lot of these hospital cup matches,' remembers Geoffrey. 'I'd be working on the farm, and someone would come round to ask if I could play, and I'd get out the bicycle, strap my bat and pads on the cross-bar, and cycle anything up to ten miles to play. The Yorkshire village wickets were good and the cricket was keen. After I'd made a few thirties and forties I got the odd match with Dad and Eric for Londesborough Park.' He was of rather less sturdy build than Eric and Bill, and here on the Yorkshire wolds he further developed the wiry toughness of mind and body that was to be so important to him later.

1933 was a year of decision for Bill. The Christmas term was to be his last; at the end of it he would have to decide about his future. Was he going to be good enough for first-class cricket? In an early-season friendly against Suffolk at Lowestoft, Falcon put him in first-wicket-down and he made 92; but Suffolk had no status then and did not enter the minor counties competition until the following year. Yet the first day's play, and his own undoubted success in it, brought him into an atmosphere of conviviality and adulation that was irresistible to a seventeen-year-old. Creeping back into the dormitory that night long after lights out – scarcely the last time, as he would readily admit, that he was to have a late night in the middle of a cricket match – he found his Headmaster rather more tolerant than a certain chairman of selectors was later to prove. But was his

Eric and Bill in their
Bracondale School days;
below, Burlingham Cricket
Club, 1887, with the young
Harry Edrich bottom left

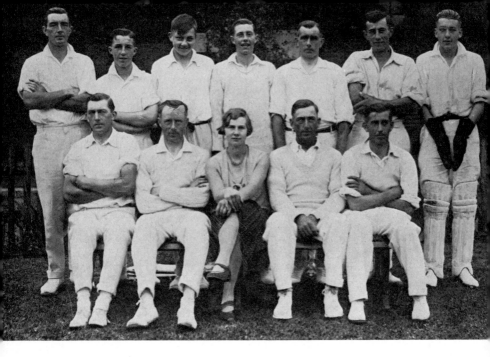

The first All-Edrich XI, Blofield, 1932: back row, l to r, Fred, Bill Jnr., George Jnr., Eric, Arthur Snr., John, Arthur; front, Charlie, George Snr., Cis, Edwin and Harry M.; *below*, W.J., Harry and W.A. at the 1938 All-Edrich match, also at Blofield

success against Suffolk significant? Another **pair** of spectacles in the next Norfolk match made him doubt it, and although he played in ten matches in the competition that year, and proved a useful member of the side, his record was not outstanding, both his batting and bowling averages being about 20.

With his short, swiftly accelerating run, his catapult-type slinging action, and the follow-through that seemed likely to propel him down the wicket in the wake of the ball, he was still generating exceptional pace for his age and size – so much so that in a Club and Ground match Jack Nichols took the gloves away from the 15-year-old Bryan Stevens, later to become the regular Norfolk wicket-keeper, and kept wicket himself. But during that season Bill had his first close-up of a really great batsman when George Headley played at Lakenham for the West Indies, and he could not get a ball past him. Headley made 257 not out, and Bill, opening the bowling, sent down 13 overs and took 0 for 61. The visit of the West Indies followed straight after the 'bodyline' tour, and Martindale was ready to give English batsmen a taste of it. He broke one Norfolk batsman's jaw, his first ball to Bill parted his hair, and although Bill stood up to him and made 35 he was kept strictly on the defensive. It was his first glimpse since Mohammed Nissar of what real pace meant.

During that season, however, he also had glimpses of a number of players of about his own age who were on the threshold of a cricket career, young men like Len Hutton, Norman Yardley, Arthur Fagg, and Doug Wright; and although he realised that Hutton and Fagg, particularly, were far ahead of him in development, the comparison did not depress him unduly. If they could do it, he felt, so could he.

1933, as it happened, was a great year for Norfolk cricket, as they topped the championship table. Their best win was against Buckinghamshire, the previous year's champions, at Lakenham, and Bill got 55 not out in the second innings and made the winning hit. He was now batting regularly at No. 3, and after this match Falcon presented him with his county cap. He was still thinking his future over when autumn came, and he went on working for the degree that would open the doors to a teaching career; but by the Christmas holidays he had made up his mind.

He still had to screw up the courage to broach the matter to his father; and for once he found that understanding parent unresponsive. Sacrifices had been made so that he could complete his education. They had not been made so that he could become a professional cricketer. What would his future be at thirty-five or forty? Why not get his degree first? But Bill senior knew in his heart that it was a losing battle, and secretly he was not displeased.

The ambitious young cricketer of those days was at a serious disadvantage if he was born or lived in a minor county. In default of a birth or residential qualification for a first-class county, a two-year apprenticeship had to be served. And since Norfolk was surrounded by minor counties, Bill would have to go some distance afield. He chose Northamptonshire, partly because it was the nearest first-class county, partly because in those days it was one of the weakest, which he felt would give him a better chance. But even Northants did not get excited at the prospect of signing a young hopeful of such modest achievement, and they suggested he apply again later.

Rejecting his father's advice to give up, Bill talked to Jack Nichols, who consulted Michael Falcon. Few people care to be responsible for advising others to take chances with their lives, and Falcon was no exception. 'I can get you into the Norwich Union,' he said. 'No,' said Bill, 'I want to be a professional cricketer. I've already written to Northants.' Seeing that the boy was determined, Falcon changed his ground. Cricketers, he believed, were apt to go unnoticed in the provinces. They should aspire to play at Headquarters, where the scribes were, and where they were continually under the eye of the people who mattered. 'Leave it to me,' he said. Next time he went to a committee meeting at Lord's he spoke to Billy Findlay, the MCC secretary. 'Hendren and Hearne can't last for ever,' he said. 'You'll be needing one or two young batsmen to take their place. Now this lad Edrich . . .' So it was settled. Bill was to go to Lord's for a trial in April 1934. If accepted, he would join the MCC second-class ground staff but would be available to play for Norfolk during the qualification period.

For the rest of that winter Bill worked on the farm at Woodhouse Grange, but he found it hard to keep his mind on his job. Just before the trial he damaged a hand so badly through not attending to what he was doing that only devoted nursing by Edith Edrich enabled him to go at all. Even then his hand was extremely painful. But he batted correctly, and bowled fast enough to make Ronnie Aird, the assistant secretary, hurry his shots. The revelation afterwards of his damaged hand did his chances no harm. He joined contemporaries like Syd Brown, Jack Robertson, Laurie Gray, Jack Young, and Denis Compton, all of whom, like himself, were trying to make their way in the game, and he suffered none of the homesickness that was later to afflict his cousin John.

1934, with the Australians visiting Lord's four times, to play the MCC, Middlesex, England and the Gentlemen of England in that order, gave Bill his first sight of first-class and Test cricket. But with Middlesex fielding three, four, five and some-times six amateurs, the prospects for the young professional were none too promising. There was consolation for Bill in repre-senting MCC at Oxford in his first first-class match, scoring 55 and putting on 152 with Bill Farrimond, the Lancashire reserve wicket-keeper; and later, in his first appearance at Lord's, against Cambridge University, he batted No. 6 and scored 63. He also played in some of the 'out' matches, though like Denis Compton he was apt to fret in the field if he didn't get a bowl. On the way to a game against Beaumont College the two of them got together and decided to tell Alec Waugh, the novelist, who was running the side, that they were bowlers; but they were sorry when Waugh won the toss on a perfect wicket and they found themselves Nos. 10 and 11. They managed to save their faces by putting on 60 for the last wicket (for Alex Waugh and the schoolboys, a first glimpse of a partnership that was to become historic), but it was poetic – or perhaps literary – justice when Waugh himself bowled the College out.

The enormous advance that Bill had made since the previous year was demonstrated in his games for Norfolk. In eleven innings he scored 527 runs, with a highest score of 138 and an average of 47, and he began to bowl really fast, if without much guile as yet, topping the county averages with 40 wickets at 12.87 each. It looked very much as though he was ready for the first-class game, yet he still had another season to go before he could play for Middlesex. It seemed a waste, but he would just have to learn all he could in the meantime.

Another Edrich who had made up his mind long since that he would never stop learning was Bill senior, and the 1934 season brought him a new experience when he got his first hundred. The Londesborough Park ground lay in a hollow on the top of the wolds, and it was, according to the centurion himself, 'as pretty a ground as a man'd ever want to see, and a lovely wicket. The slopes around were covered with heather, and beyond that was a set of trees. It was an easy ground to score on, but that particular day was a sort of festival day with the club, and we had a good side against us down from Hull, with a very fast bowler from the Yorkshire Council. I was No. 4 or 5, and just before lunch somebody got out, and I went in to join Eric. He got out last ball before lunch, caught in the slips, and I think I was 3 not out. We had a good lunch, with a flagon of beer, and after lunch we played carefully at first, until we got on top of the bowling. When I'd made 50 I tried to retire to give the others a chance, and I started walking towards the pavilion, but they shouted at me to go back, so I did. I hit the Yorkshire Council bowler for 20 in one over, four fours and two twos, and I got to 98, then took two cheeky singles. I was forty-three at the time, coming up to forty-four.' All this was accompanied by gleeful and conspiratorial exclamations from Edith.

By the end of that summer at Lord's Denis and Bill had struck up a firm friendship, and when Bill began to look round for a job to see him through the winter, he naturally thought of professional football. Denis, already on Arsenal's books, 'made it sound easy', according to Bill, and with Joe Hulme playing regularly for Arsenal, and Patsy Hendren an ex-Brentford

36

player, he was encouraged to write to one or two London clubs for a trial. This led to an interview at White Hart Lane in September 1934, a trial game in the reserves, and a contract to join the Tottenham nursery at Northfleet.

When Bill Edrich senior first saw the farm at Woodhouse Grange he had told the agents it wanted draining. 'Well, drain it,' they said. 'If you can improve the farm, do so, we want to let it.' He proceeded to do the job too well for his own security; one of his cricket friends came along, admired the farm, and hired it, and once again he was looking for a job. The agents found him a farm of 500 acres at Heacham, near Hunstanton, so he went down to see it. It was in a worse state than Woodhouse Grange had been, but the land was basically good and in the autumn of 1934 he took it over. Thus, after eighteen months in Yorkshire, the family returned to Norfolk life and Norfolk cricket.

Bill had only one MCC match that season, against Cambridge University in June, when he renewed a nodding acquaintance with Norman Yardley, later to become one of his firmest friends in the game. The pitch had not recovered from the effects of heavy rain and in a low-scoring game Bill batted only once, at No. 8, and was out cheaply, stumped, to the young West Indian leg-spinner J. H. Cameron. He bowled ten overs in the match and picked up one wicket, that of Norman Yardley, lbw – hardly an auspicious start to their friendship.

For Norfolk in the championship he played 15 innings and made 488 runs, with a highest score of 152, and took 27 wickets; but a batting average of 32 and a bowling average of 23 stimulated the comment in *Wisden* that he 'had not fared so successfully as in 1934'. So on figures alone he seemed to have gone back. But this left altogether out of account a really spectacular performance in July at Norwich against the South African tourists immediately before the third Test.

Three of South Africa's leading Test Match bowlers were playing, and when Norfolk won the toss and batted, the tall opening bowler R. J. 'Bob' Crisp, swinging the new ball and making it lift awkwardly, soon had the openers back in the pavilion. But Bill, joined by M. R. Barton, who after the war captained Surrey, settled in and eventually put on 146 with Barton, whose share was 59. Bill was in the nervous nineties when Barton got out – only he wasn't nervous. As soon as he got through his first over that morning, so he said afterwards, he knew he was going to make runs; now his hundred was in the bag and he knew that too. Every national newspaper enthused about his innings next morning, and this performance, more than anything he had done previously, established him in the minds of cricket followers as a young player with a future. 'Cutting, driving, and hooking in fine style,' said one report, 'he made 111 out of 194 in two hours and three-quarters without anything like a serious mistake.'

Towards the end of that 1935 season, Bill was joined in the Norfolk side by his elder brother Eric. Apart from his one game for the Club and Ground when he was eighteen, in which he had failed, Eric had not made much impression on Norfolk cricket, but during his two seasons in Yorkshire he had matured to such an extent that he had graduated into the Yorkshire Council and made two centuries for York. Returning to Norfolk at the age of twenty-one to play for Heacham, he began to score so consistently, and in such a compact, copybook style, that notice was taken, and an innings of 91 not out against the strong East Dereham side added the final note of conviction. He played in two matches for Norfolk that year and made 25 in the first and 34 not out and 18 in the second, a satisfactory enough start. So the following season held great promise for the cricketing Edriches.

Another young player who completed three innings in the minor counties competition that year was the seventeen-year-old Denis Compton – 12, 12 and 11. But his promise was obvious, and his chance in the county side was expected to come in 1936. Bill, two years older, and far ahead of Denis in development, was even more anxious to get started in the three-day game. But before he packed up his gear at Lord's at the end of that 1935 season to return to professional football, he was summoned to the office of the MCC secretary. There a bombshell was dropped by Billy Findlay that might have turned a young man of different temperament against Lord's and all it represented for life. Not knowing what was coming, and reflecting that a new era was about to begin for him, he bounced in to the office cheerfully enough. But he saw as he entered that Findlay, seated somewhat portentously at his desk, was putting on a serious face.

'Hello, young man. You realise you won't be qualified for Middlesex next season, don't you?'

'No, I didn't sir. Why?'

'It's simply a question of registration. We didn't receive the forms from the Norfolk secretary until October 1934. Therefore you won't be qualified until October 1936.'

'But sir, everybody knew this was why I was here.'

'Yes, I know, young man, but I'm afraid that's it.'

'Can't something be done?'

'No, nothing.' Findlay turned back to his papers, and then, to confirm that the interview was over, looked up again and said brightly: 'Good-bye.'

Bill's first reaction was that the matter ought to be investigated, and that there must be some way of putting it right. The intention had been known, the rules of qualification had been complied with, and it was simply a matter of a mistake in the paper work, for which he could not conceivably be blamed. But these were autocratic days, the secretary of an august body had spoken, and for a young professional cricketer trying to make his way in the game, outside the county of his birth, it was not wise to argue.

It had been bad enough to have to wait two years. Now, utterly deflated, he had to find some way of adjusting himself to this bitterest of disappointments. Fortunately he was not of a rebellious nature, neither was he jealous of the chances others might get that would be denied him. It would not, as it happened, be the only time in his career that the authorities would deal him a cruel blow, and now, as later, he took it philosophically. What effect it was to have on his subsequent career, though, is a matter for consideration.

There was one consolation: he was now on the MCC first-class staff. If he took his medicine, he might make a few first-class appearances for MCC. And he would presumably be allowed to play another season for Norfolk. That, surely, could not be denied him. With the winter's soccer to look forward to, his natural optimism returned. He would make the best of it.

He had been given a broad hint that he might be wanted by the Spurs that season in the League side, but he got one chance only, against Blackpool at White Hart Lane in October, when Welsh international Willie Evans, the regular outside-left, was ill. 'It fell to me to take a corner kick,' he wrote afterwards, 'and the ball fell nicely at Morrison's boot and he volleyed it into the net, and said an encouraging word to me as he went up-field for a fresh centre.' An encouraging word, forsooth! Other times, other manners. Two more goals came direct from his centres, and there were flattering reports on his play in the Sunday papers. 'Fine new Spur!' said one headline. 'Edrich has arrived in the Spurs first team to stay there.' But the following Saturday Willie Evans was fit again, and Bill was back in the reserves. Evans, of course, was a great winger; but he was careful not to fall ill again that season.

So to the 1936 season, and the emergence of Denis Compton as a great player in the making. Coming into the Middlesex side for the Whitsun match against Sussex at Lord's, he completed 1,000 runs in his first season, averaging 35, which put him second only to Hendren among the regulars, and drew from 'Plum' Warner the tribute that he was 'the best young batsman who has come out since Walter Hammond was a boy'. To watch the success of this young man two years his junior who had had the good sense to be born in Middlesex, and to watch it from a straitjacket of red tape, must have been galling indeed for Bill; but he was never jealous of Denis, and in fact never felt he needed to be. Denis was something special, a genius; and in addition to that he was a friend. Each took delight in the other's feats. And curiously enough, in that baptismal season of Denis's in which he drew so much acclaim, far more astonishing were the figures of Bill Edrich.

His opportunities in first-class cricket were restricted to nine innings, but in them he scored three hundreds, a century in every three visits to the wicket, a proportion normally exclusive to Bradman. For the first MCC match, against Yorkshire at the beginning of May, he was not selected, but for the second, against Surrey, he went in No. 3 and stayed while 363 runs were added for the next three wickets. His biggest partnership was with Patsy Hendren, and Patsy, at forty-seven, dominated it completely. Here surely is the perfect answer to those who doubt whether the great players of yesterday would dominate the game today. Of their partnership of 297, Hendren made 202. After Alf Gover and Eddie Watts had been worn down, the Surrey bowling was friendly enough, and the wicket was good, but the audacious batting came from Hendren. He made his double century in three hours and hit twenty-nine 4's. Bill's comment? 'As usual when batting on a beautiful wicket with someone with a lot of experience, one didn't see an awful lot of the strike.'

Hendren could count up to six, and did. Bill could count up to six, but daren't. Grinning at him down the wicket, Patsy seemed to say: 'You know, young man, in a season or two it'll be all yours. But they've come to watch me today.' 'That,' says Bill, 'was fair enough. I was watching the master.'

Thus Bill's first century in first-class cricket – 114 – was overshadowed by the brilliance of his partner; but after Surrey had batted and then followed on, they set MCC 94 to win, at which point Gover and Watts bowled flat out. They got two down for 16, which brought Patsy in again to join Bill. Teasing Alf Gover by adopting an old-fashioned stance, head back, left toe cocked, he failed to avoid the bouncer he was asking for and had to retire. It was left to Bill (51 not out) to see MCC home.

Six weeks later, against Oxford University, Bill was batting again with Patsy, putting on 141 this time in 85 minutes. Patsy got 98 and Bill 114. This time Bill was not outshone. 'Edrich hit magnificently all round the wicket,' said *Wisden*.

The leveller came ten days later against Cambridge, when Jehangir Khan, flinging the ball down at a lively pace off a short run, made one leave him as he went forward and he dragged his foot, recording his first duck in first-class cricket.

His third century came against Kent at the Folkestone Festival on the last day of August, after a first-innings duck. The wicket favoured the seam bowlers, and it was Watt who got Bill both times. In the second innings he had his first look at the wiles of 'Tich' Freeman, and he went down the wicket from the start to meet his flighted slows. A hundred at the second go, after a first-innings duck, was to become something of a habit with Bill, saying something, surely, about his character.

No doubt Bill's place in the first-class averages that year – ahead of all other batsmen except Wally Hammond, and not very far behind him – flattered him a little. MCC matches were 'friendlies' in a sense, and some of the pressures of the county championship were no doubt missing. But they are surely a guide to what he might have done if it had been the full first-class season he had deserved. He also had a high place – sixth – in the second-class averages, scoring 397 runs for Norfolk, with one century, for an average of 44. He bowled very little for MCC, but sent down 121 overs for Norfolk and took 16 wickets for 20 runs each.

Eric played six innings for Norfolk that year, but only in one of them, when he scored 86, did he show his best form. He was still scoring heavily for Heacham, however, as were both his younger brother Geoffrey and his father, and he also played frequently for West Norfolk. Geoffrey at eighteen had filled out a little and was beginning to put more power into his shots, his cover-drive particularly catching the eye, and he was also becoming a useful seam bowler at about medium pace. His all-round form brought him an invitation to play with Eric for West Norfolk against Norfolk Club and Ground, and he took his chance and got 50. He was already known to Michael Falcon and Jack Nichols, they saw the innings, and with Nichols on the verge of retirement, Geoffrey was offered terms as the new Norfolk professional. It was just what he wanted, and he could hardly believe his luck.

That winter, Bill got a regular place in the Spurs League side until mid-October, when an ankle injury put him out of the game for the rest of the season, threatening to spoil the 1937 cricket season for him as well. This, after the frustrations of the previous summer, seemed an intolerable prospect. Fortunately a manipulative operation put the ankle right just in time, and in May he began the career for Middlesex that was to span the next twenty-two years. Both he and Denis ran into form in the early MCC matches, but they did nothing outstanding for Middlesex until early June, when Bill made his first hundred for his adopted county, against Lancashire at Lord's. The match, which ended on a note of great excitement, was a triumph for Bill. Batting first, Lancashire made 233 (Jack Iddon 114). Iddon's display, however, according to *Wisden,* 'was surpassed by Edrich, whose straight driving, cutting and leg-side strokes were superb'. He made 175 of Middlesex's 369, which left Lancashire 136 behind. With Norman Oldfield (65) leading a recovery, Middlesex were eventually set 174 to win, on a wicket that was now affected by rain. When they lost six wickets for 33 the game looked over. But Bill, who had bowled 18 overs in Lancashire's second innings and then gone almost straight in to bat, was still there, playing the first of countless innings for Middlesex in which he was to show a technique against the turning or lifting ball that was the equal, if not the superior, of anyone else in England. He got some help from the tail, especially from the giant hitter Jim Smith, who made 33, and when Gray, the last man in, joined him, only 20-odd were needed. Gray was then run out in trying to give Bill the strike, and Bill was left high and dry with 73 not out.

Everything that had been predicted about Compton and Edrich came true in that 1937 summer, and in the last of the three Test Matches against New Zealand, Denis played and did well. Hutton and Washbrook also played in this series, but Bill, who was to join them to form England's first line of offence and defence in post-war Test cricket, was not chosen. Yet he scored over 2,000 runs in his first full season, and on the whole, as *Wisden* said, 'was more consistent than Denis, if not quite so attractive to watch'. This kind of comparison was to dog Bill throughout his career, and many found it inadequate, since few batsmen were as stimulating to watch as Bill. Although his strength on the leg side could hardly be over-emphasized, the repetition of it suggested that he was a leg side player, whereas he had all the shots and used them.

The last match of the season, Middlesex v. Surrey, was especially memorable for being Patsy Hendren's last game, although as it happened it ended in farce. The Surrey attack suffered another long exposure to the destructive skills of Patsy and Bill, but as the Surrey batsmen had already amassed a total of 509, somebody had to make runs in reply, and after two wickets had fallen cheaply, they put on 182. No one played the slow bowlers better than Patsy, even at the age of forty-eight, and his footwork was still a delight to watch. Bill made 96 and Patsy 103, and on the last day Middlesex were set 295 to win. At 178 for seven Errol Holmes, the Surrey captain, aiming to give away 22 runs quickly so as to get the new ball (taken then at 200), bowled an over of byes and wides in which no one made any effort to prevent the ball going through to the boundary. The crowd bellowed its disapproval, Gubby Allen and Walter Robins, who were batting, added to the fun by appealing against the light although the sun was shining, and Bill Reeves, that most fertile of umpires in anecdote, promptly removed the bails to bring the farce to an end.

In Denis Compton's first year, Jack Hearne had played in only one or two matches before giving up; now, at the end of Bill's first year, the other half of that great combination was retiring, and after twenty-five years of Hendren and Hearne it was to be Compton and Edrich. Bill and Denis have both paid tribute to them, especially of course to Patsy; both felt they had benefited a great deal from playing with him day by day for at least a full season. He advised them how to play certain bowlers, and told them what they carried in their repertoire, which was especially useful in their first season or so, when they knew so

44

few of them. But he did not expect them to take his advice too seriously. 'Don't worry about the name of the bowler,' he would say, 'try to see the maker's name on the ball.'

'He was a great mover of his feet,' says Bill, 'and watching him come down the wicket, one tried to move one's feet in the same way. You can learn a lot from watching someone like him at close quarters. Patsy was not at all resentful of our arrival in the side and was wonderfully helpful. The greatest thing I learned from Patsy was to play my shots in the direction in which the ball was swinging or turning, to play with the tide. Of course there are wickets on which one can safely cut the off-spinner, but if the ball was turning I always played it round to leg.

'Patsy was a great hooker, too, and there were several quick bowlers about in those days, men like Copson, Gover, Farnes, Wellard, and Clark, of Northants, who I thought was a thrower. There was Bill Bowes, too, and although he wasn't really quick he was awkward. Most players move inside the line to hook, and the ball goes behind square leg, generally in the air. Patsy would get in line, body behind the ball, and thump it to square leg or even mid-wicket, turning his wrists over as he did so. He played the ball down, and I aimed to do the same. If the ball lifts one can take avoiding action, swaying out of the way. Of course every now and again you get hit, as I did, but you get hit far less often if you keep your eye on the ball.'

Just as Bill truly arrived in first-class cricket that season, so Eric, at the age of twenty-three, finally established himself in the Norfolk side. In 13 innings he scored 443 runs for an average of 49, and he made his first century, 161 against Hertfordshire at Cokenach. He also, quite by chance, took up wicket-keeping. Hitherto, both for Heacham and for West Norfolk, he had bowled medium-paced out-swingers. But one day at Heacham the wicket-keeper was injured, and the skipper singled out Eric as the most likely substitute. He had, of course, watched his father keeping wicket all his cricketing life, and he dropped into the job naturally and easily. Indeed it might be said that he dropped into it with a flourish, since even at this early stage he kept with a show of style. Perhaps he copied his father's mannerisms. Anyway a few days later he kept in a match to Wilfred Thompson, the Norfolk fast bowler, reckoned to be one of the fastest in the country at that time, and when the regular Norfolk wicket-keeper had a car accident soon afterwards he found himself filling the role of wicket-keeper-batsman for the county.

It was an exciting summer, too, for Geoffrey – his first as a professional cricketer. In April he went into digs with Jack Nichols in Norwich, he bowled at the members for five hours a day three days a week, he played for the Club and Ground, he helped Jack Nichols with the coaching, learning a lot himself while doing so, and very sensibly the Norfolk Committee played him in the Minor Counties competition to give him experience. In 13 innings he made no scores over 30, but he showed a sound defence and some pleasing shots, and he proved a hard man to get out on any kind of wicket. The Norfolk committee saw him as an investment for the future, and they watched his progress with interest.

There was another notable arrival, too, in that summer of 1937. Fred, the youngest of Harry Edrich's sons, and now thirty-two, had married a Blofield girl called Ena Rope, and on 21st June their first son, John Hugh, was born at Blofield.

When he first signed forms for the Spurs, Bill had got them to concede that, for him, cricket must always come first, and when, in the winter of 1937–38, the chance came to tour India with a team under the sponsorship and captaincy of Lord Tennyson, he accepted, realising that it meant good-bye to big football. Denis, on the other hand, elected to continue his football career with Arsenal. Percy Chapman, Wally Hammond and Tom Goddard also declined invitations, and Yorkshire wouldn't let Maurice Leyland make the trip; but it was still an immensely strong side, probably the best to tour India up to that time. A lot of the games were played on matting, and Bill found the conditions quite different from anything he was used to, but he

46

adapted himself readily and topped the averages both for the five unofficial Tests and for all matches. He also made a name for himself, surprisingly to those who only saw him post-war, as an outfield. He was fortunate, though, that his constitution, and especially his stomach, was proof against the many ailments that beset the others.

It was on this tour that he cemented his friendship with Norman Yardley. Yardley was Bill's type of cricketer, a fighter, and rather more open in his approach to the game, perhaps, than the average Yorkshireman. Like Bill a sociable character, he shared another Edrich quality – he was never heard to say anything unpleasant about anybody.

The tour of India ended in February. Then it was back to England to get ready for the 1938 Australians.

Right from the first day of the season, Saturday, 30th April, things went right for Bill. Opening for MCC that evening after Yorkshire had been put out for 339, he soon lost his partner, but next day he and Denis continued in a stand of 146. Bill eventually made 104, but he had no chance to bat again as the last day was washed out. Against Surrey, again for MCC, he made 37 and 115, and then, when Middlesex began their programme at Lord's on Saturday, 7th May against Warwickshire, he got 63 and 20 not out. The next game, against Gloucestershire, brought him 182 and 71, most of them off Tom Goddard and Reg Sinfield (Goddard 12 for 276, Sinfield 3 for 285), and then he quietened down with 31 and 53 not out for MCC against the Australians (his first sight of O'Reilly), and 45 and 15 for Middlesex against Lancashire. He had thus made 736 runs in the first three weeks of the season, all at Lord's, and he had three more matches, also at Lord's, to get the 264 he wanted for 1,000 runs before the end of May. When he made 245 of them in one innings against Nottinghamshire (Larwood and Voce included) on 21st and 23rd May, all that was left was the formality of scoring another 19 runs in five possible innings to reach the target. Notts in fact were beaten by an innings, but that still left four.

In the first of these matches, against Worcestershire, he

opened the batting to the bowling of Bob Crisp, one of the South Africans against whom he had made a hundred three years earlier for Norfolk. He forced the first ball of the match back hard past the bowler, only to see Crisp reach down to his left and make an incredible one-handed catch. Middlesex were all out for 241, yet they won again by an innings, and that was one match gone. The second match was Middlesex against the Australians, beginning on Saturday, 28th May.

The previous day, at Southampton, Bradman had completed 1,000 runs before the end of May for the second time in his career. The feat was behind him. Bill still needed 19. And when it rained all day Saturday and Sunday, his opportunities had been reduced, almost certainly, to a single innings. Bradman won the toss and batted, but in conditions that were strange to them the Australians did not show to advantage and were all out for 132. Bad light and showers further reduced the playing time, and when Edrich finally got to the crease that evening he was confronted by McCormick and O'Reilly.

Almost at once, Price was lbw to McCormick and W. H. Webster was caught behind. That brought Denis in. But Bill was making heavy weather of O'Reilly. Ever since his early coaching from Jack Nichols he had always tried to read spin bowlers from the hand. Indeed he had been taught to watch the approach of all types of bowler carefully. 'You can start looking for what's coming as soon as the bowler starts to run up,' Nichols would say. 'You can see from the way he's holding the ball what the delivery's likely to be.' He was trying to do this with O'Reilly, but without success. Even at the moment of delivery he was still uncertain.

O'Reilly was an over-spinner. Although the ball was always coming from the back of the hand, he never really bowled a genuine leg-spinner. They were all top-spinners, bowled at near medium pace and liable to go a bit either way. And consequently they all bounced. This was why he always bowled to two very close short-legs. And because he didn't really tweak the ball, he had far more control than the average leg-break bowler, so that he very rarely bowled a bad ball.

Finding that the hand came over so quickly that he couldn't read the spin, Bill made up his mind to play O'Reilly off the pitch. But when he had scored 9 he missed a googly and was bowled.

It was a great many runs, 990, yet in the record books it didn't mean a thing. There was one more day, Tuesday, 31st May, but the weather was still unsettled, and in any case Middlesex had a lot of batting to come. Then it would be the Australians' turn again.

Next morning Bill watched in puzzled admiration as Compton, Robins and Human all punished O'Reilly, three times hitting him for six. Bad light and showers caused further interruptions, but Middlesex eventually gained a lead of 56. With two-and-a-half hours left for play, there was nothing for the Australians to do but to bat out time.

There was a dramatic start as Nevell bowled Badcock for a duck. But Fingleton, Bradman and McCabe saw to it that there was no collapse, and with less than half an hour to go the game was petering out into the inevitable draw. Then Bradman, who was 30 not out, suddenly turned for the pavilion.

He was declaring. The Australians were only 58 ahead, and he was declaring. With only 20 minutes' playing time left, he could not hope to bowl out a boys' team, let alone Middlesex. There was more chance, perhaps, for Middlesex to get the 10 runs an over they would need to win; but it was a remote one. No, the gesture could have only one meaning. He was giving Bill the chance to get his 1,000 runs after all.

As Bill walked out to the middle, he passed the Don. 'We're not giving these to you, Bill,' he said. 'You've got to get 'em.'

No doubt he meant it – up to a point. But this time he did not start with McCormick and O'Reilly. He gave the ball to McCabe and Waite. Robins, for his part, chose as Bill's partner the one player who could never be tied down at one end – Denis.

Ten minutes later, Bradman was shaking hands with Bill at the wicket. The Don had a heart after all.

Bill had only two more innings before the first Test at Not-

49

tingham, but he scored runs in both. Then he went to Trent Bridge, and there his misfortunes began.

In the first Test O'Reilly bowled him his faster ball. It was the first time he'd seen it, he came down late on it, and he played it on to his boot and thence on to his wicket. England made 658 for eight, however, so his failure was scarcely noticed. In the second Test he was out cheaply twice through trying to hook too early, and when he was selected again for the third Test there were mutterings in the Midlands and the North about favouritism at Headquarters. But this third Test, due to be played at Old Trafford, was washed out completely, and he was retained for the fourth. Meanwhile Ken Farnes, angry at being left out of the side for Old Trafford, bowled so fast in the Gentlemen *v.* Players match at Lord's that he knocked Bill out. The ball brushed his glove as he played back protectively, and when he came round a minute or so later he found he was out, caught off glove and temple in the gully. This was the occasion when Fred Price, sent in as nightwatchman after Bill's dismissal, tipped the ball obligingly into the slips before entering his famous plea about having a wife and kids.

Bill, as so often in his career, quickly demonstrated his powers of recovery, and in the fourth Test at Leeds, where the wicket took spin from the start, he was one of the few England batsmen to play O'Reilly and Fleetwood-Smith with any certainty. For this he was retained for the final Test at the Oval; but again he failed.

Sixty-seven runs in six Test Match innings, with an average of 11, put Bill last but one in the England averages; and his May average of 90 fell to 52 by the end of the season. Perhaps the most remarkable thing is that he continued to score, in county cricket, as heavily as he did. In his partnerships with Denis for Middlesex he was rarely overshadowed, and when they put on 163 against Warwickshire, Denis's share was 58. Yet so far as his international career was concerned he had raised serious doubts about his temperament, doubts which were to haunt him for many years.

Could temperament really have been the reason for his failures? It is true that he was unlucky in the Tests that year; but when a batsman appears to be consistently unlucky, some other reason must be looked for. The most likely explanation, perhaps, is that by the end of May he was mentally and physically drained, and that some reaction was inevitable. The experience of Glenn Turner in 1973 strikes an interesting parallel; after getting 1,000 runs by the end of May on the New Zealand tour, he averaged only 23 in five Test Match innings and was unrecognisable as the player who later in the same season scored 1,000 runs for Worcestershire.

To say that success came suddenly to Bill, after only one full season in first-class cricket, would need some qualification; but it is substantially true. Despite his five seasons with Norfolk, he did not really come up the hard way, in that he missed the two or three seasons of acclimatisation that bring most young players on. The spotlight was on him, but something in his education was lacking. Somewhere here may lie the germ of his spectacular Test Match failures of 1938.

Of Bill's brothers, the one who made the most solid advance that year was Geoffrey. Gaining in confidence, he made 293 runs in 16 innings for Norfolk, with a top score of 63 and an average of 21, and he bowled 202 overs of medium-paced out-swingers and took 26 wickets at 18 runs each, to become one of the county's leading bowlers. Indeed it was for a performance with the ball – nine wickets at Lakenham in the match against Bucks – that he was awarded his county cap.

Eric, now established as the regular Norfolk wicket-keeper, also had a successful season, making 320 runs in 12 innings and averaging just under 30. His best innings was 110 against Hertfordshire at Sawbridgeworth. But before that, in May, he represented the Minor Counties at Oxford against the University in his first first-class match. Played as a batsman ('Hopper' Levett kept wicket), he went in No. 3 and made 25 and 6. In the same side was a young 20-year-old whom he was to get to know particularly well in later years – John Ikin, then playing for Staffordshire.

The youngest of the four brothers, Brian, whose schooling had ended, as Eric's and Geoffrey's had done, at fourteen, and who was now learning to train greyhounds for a living, got into the Heacham side that summer when not yet sixteen after a season in the Seconds, and he established himself as a useful bowler of off-cutters and a middle to late order batsman.

An end of the season game at Blofield was not without its significance: on Wednesday 14th September, Michael Falcon brought down a Norfolk side to play an All-Edrich XI. The match was suggested by the local Rector to raise funds for a new recreation ground. Bill agreed to form the Edrich XI, with his father as captain, and Jack Nichols was deputed to prepare a wicket. Despite his Test Match failures – even partly because of them – there was no more popular cricketer in the country than Bill, certainly not in Norfolk, and the novelty of such a game attracted the interest of the national Press and the BBC, who sent along an outside broadcast team. 'W.J. out first ball,' was the headline next day, and indeed Bill, opening with his father, was caught Rought-Rought bowled Pilch first ball of the innings. Not surely in any score book would one find, in one line, a more distinguished combination of Norfolk cricketing names. Michael Falcon had declared his own side's innings closed so that Bill would be at the wicket for the broadcast, but he got out before it went on the air. The rest of the game was spoiled by rain.

Here is how the team was made up: William Arthur, farmer; Edwin Harry, farmer; George Herbert, auctioneer; Harry Macdonald, haulage contractor; Eric Harry, farm mechanic; William John, Middlesex; Geoffrey Arthur, Norfolk; Brian Robert, greyhound trainer; Arthur Edwin, hospital attendant; George Charles, auctioneer's clerk; and Alan Walter, engineer. Four of the original nine sons, and seven of the grandsons. Altogether there were more than thirty of the Edrich family present, and proudest of the lot was grandfather Harry Edrich, still as mobile as ever in his wheelchair at 70.

Alice Underdown – she had duly married her cricketer boy-friend – was scoring as before, helped, or perhaps hindered, by her four-year-old son.

This match led to another a few days later, when the Edriches got together a second time to play in a match at Barton Hall. The owner, a character named Michael Trubshawe immortalised by David Niven in *The Moon's a Balloon*, had organised a fête and cricket festival, and he got a useful side together to do battle with the Edrich clan. In this match young Brian Edrich, a month past his sixteenth birthday, made 60, and he batted with such composure that someone who saw his innings mentioned his name to Kent. A few weeks later Brian had a letter from the secretary asking if he was prepared to join the Kent staff. He was not even asked to go for a trial. Like Bill and Geoffrey, Brian was determined on a cricket career, and the Kent committee found him a winter job with Whitbreads in Canterbury so that he could start his residential qualification at once. As it happened, the MCC then brought in a scheme for special registration, and although it was too late to save the locust years for Bill, Kent took advantage of it to register Brian.

Meanwhile the touring party for South Africa had been chosen, and to the general surprise Bill was in it. He learned afterwards that there were interminable discussions before the decision was made, and that only Wally Hammond's faith in him, particularly his respect for his all-round ability (what Hammond called 'the bits and pieces'), saved his place. He made a moderate start to the tour, but he did well with the ball, and an injury to Hutton which kept him out of the first Test clinched Bill's place in the side. He proceeded to fail in both innings. Hutton returned for the second Test, and Bill expected the axe to fall, but he was preferred to Norman Yardley. Paul Gibb went in first with Hutton, and Bill batted No. 6 and made a duck.

Four years earlier, at Lakenham, he had got a hundred against the South Africans. Now his confidence was gone and he couldn't get a run. In the third Test he was relegated in the order to No. 7; but thanks to big innings from Hammond and Paynter he didn't have to bat. He did, however, pick up two good wickets, and with Yardley and Hugh Bartlett doing little in the intervening matches he kept his place for the fourth Test. But yet another batting failure, and no wickets to redeem it, seemed to make his further retention impossible. From the accusation of favouritism at Lord's he now laboured under the soubriquet of 'Hammond's pet'. Yet in the next match, against Natal, he carried the MCC batting with a superb 150, and for the final Test at Durban he could not be left out.

The story of that match can be briefly told. South Africa 530; England 316 (Edrich fails again). South Africa 481; England set 696 to win.

Despite his sociable temperament, Bill had cut out the parties during the Test Matches, and this contributed to the tension he was under. That evening 'Tuppy' Owen-Smith, with whom Bill had played for Middlesex, invited him to a party, and he went. It lasted until late, and the drink was champagne. Next morning, as England began their hopeless task, Hammond strolled across to Bill. 'I'm going to put you in first wicket down, Bill. This is your last chance in the series.' Except when opening with Hutton at the start of the tour, all his best scores had been made from No. 3, and he regarded it as his natural place in the order. 'You can make runs, Bill, if you try,' continued Hammond. 'Don't be afraid to go for the ball if you can see it.' Then he grinned. 'If you can make a couple of hundred we might stand a chance.' And that, of course, is exactly what Bill did.

Paradoxically, after persevering with him through two successive Test Match series and finally having their faith confirmed, the England selectors now cast him aside. When the West Indies toured England in 1939, England's leading batsmen were Hutton, Paynter, Hammond, Compton and Hardstaff. The last two, of course, had not been in South Africa; but there was still a place for another batsman. First Harold Gimblett, then Arthur Fagg, then Walter Keeton, were tried as partners for Hutton, but never Bill; and when Paynter was left out of the last Test his place went to Norman **Oldfield**. It was not that Bill had a poor season; far from it. He topped 2,000 runs again, made seven hundreds for Middlesex, and finished far ahead in the averages of most of those who supplanted him, so that on figures alone he should have kept his place. But he may have suffered to some extent from the revulsion felt in England, justified or not, from that Durban marathon; and certain it is that his determination to force his way back into the side lent an unwonted restraint to his batting that year. Another factor that may have weighed with Hammond, at least, was the apparent falling off in his bowling. Although he got through 185 overs that season, his 15 wickets cost him 50 runs apiece.

For his brothers, 1939 was another season of steady progress and development, and this was especially true of Geoffrey. Now twenty-one, he emerged as one of the leading batsmen in the Minor Counties, ranking with promising young northern professionals like Willie Watson and Winston Place, of Yorkshire and Lancashire Second Elevens respectively. Sixteen innings brought him 614 runs, his first century in the competition, and an average of 47, and he looked ripe for graduation to the first-class game. *His* temperament, at least, was not called into question. 'Geoffrey Edrich,' said the *Eastern Daily Press*, 'has now supplied proof of the advancement that was expected to come with experience. His repertoire of scoring strokes has been increased, and with the greater variety there has also come added power. His innings of 53 against the West Indies was rich in merit, and the century which followed at Bishop's Stortford did not surprise those who have recognised his capabilities. Edrich has the right temperament, and is not lacking in the important essentials of confidence and concentration. If he has nerves he is able to keep them under control. His innings against Hertfordshire had the additional merit of being played at a time when Norfolk were in great need of runs. It was a long fighting innings, with the goal only reached when he had batted 220 minutes, and the smile which seldom left his face suggested that he enjoyed every minute.' He was not called upon to do so much bowling, but he picked up 16 wickets at 25 runs each. Eric, too, had a good if less even record – 408 runs, average 31, highest score 169 – and like Geoffrey he had a good knock (47) against the West Indies. Consistency was not his strong point, but at times he kept wicket brilliantly.

Brian, who did not reach his seventeenth birthday until that August, was meanwhile gaining useful all-round experience with Kent II, alongside more mature players like Tom Spencer, Godfrey Evans and Ray Dovey. His record was modest, but this was all Kent expected of him at that age, and his promise was obvious.

That was the situation with the four brothers when war put an end to all first- and second-class cricket for the foreseeable future. Eric, at twenty-five, although still a farmer at heart, had become a successful member of the Norfolk side. Bill, at twenty-three, had established himself as one of the most prolific run-getters in the game, and he had played nine times for England; but he was out of favour with the selectors, and his bowling had fallen off. Geoffrey, in his third season as a professional with Norfolk, had made the break-through as a batsman in Minor Counties cricket and was looking to other horizons. Brian at seventeen had his foot on the first rung of the ladder and promised to develop into the most exciting cricketer of them all.

Towards the end of that summer, playing for Norfolk Bitternes against a side raised by Mike Trubshawe, Geoffrey got a hundred that so impressed Giles Baring, of the banking family (A. E. G. Baring, the Hampshire fast bowler, then twenty-eight), that word was passed to the Hampshire committee, resulting in the offer of an engagement with that county for 1940. A few days later Geoffrey was called up for the militia, and although Michael Falcon got him deferred until the end of the season, by the time he reported to Colchester the prospect of playing for Hampshire in 1940 had vanished. At Colchester on 18th September, Geoffrey volunteered for the RAF and was at once drafted into the infantry.

Eric found himself in much the same position as his father in the first war; above the age for immediate call-up, and in a reserved occupation. Brian was still under age, and he returned to Norfolk to work on the farm. Bill, whose preferences stood rather more chance of getting a hearing than Geoffrey's, volunteered for flying duties with the RAF.

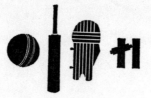

Bill, Eric, Geoffrey,
Brian and John

The outbreak of war brought, for the four Edrich brothers, much the same sense of hiatus and frustration as it did for many thousands of others. Bill, although accepted as an aircrew volunteer, waited impatiently for his call-up, and Christmas 1939 found him at home with his family in Norfolk. Geoffrey also spent his Christmas in Norfolk – with the 5th Battalion of the Royal Norfolk Regiment, mounting an anti-aircraft guard over the Royal Family at Sandringham. Eric and Brian were working on the farm. But early in 1940 Bill was given the tip that the quickest way into the flying branch was to join up in the physical fitness branch and then remuster. This he did, and after a year's training as a pilot he reported to 107 Squadron in his home county of Norfolk on 21st May 1941 to fly twin-engined bombers.

'As I walked into the spacious hall,' Bill has written of his arrival in the Officers' Mess, 'I could hear the sound of voices and the clink of glasses, and for a moment I hesitated. Up to this moment I had been a pupil, the lowest of the low, but with many hands ready to guide me. Now I was a Blenheim pilot, about to take part in the war. Would I measure up to it? What would the other fellows be like? Had I got what it takes?'

He soon found that his training days were not over after all. Practice formation flying, and practice low-level bombing, kept him busy for the next few days. In the middle of it he was selected to play cricket for the RAF against the Rest of England at Lord's. Shamefacedly he asked his CO for the day off – and got it.

In 1938 he had scored 1,000 runs by 31st May. Now it was 2nd June and he'd hardly touched a bat. He scored 6 and 1, and failed to take a wicket or a catch. Too much practice, he reflected, of the wrong kind. Three days later he was glad enough of that practice when he was briefed for his first operational flight.

For the rest of that eventful summer, Bill flew on low-level anti-shipping strikes and on the low-level bombing of enemy coastal targets. Churchill himself came to remind the squadron that the German Air Force must be diverted from other fronts, that 43,000 British civilians had been killed in air raids in the previous twelve months, and that his promise that the RAF would retaliate by day and night must now be fulfilled. The losses of the 'daylight boys', as they called themselves, were severe; but Bill survived. Before the summer was over he had been promoted to flight commander and had won the DFC.

Early in 1940 Geoffrey had married Olga Quayle, a girl born in Swaffham of Manx parents, and they had one son. But in 1941 Geoffrey, now a platoon sergeant, was posted to the Middle East. The troopship was on its way north from Cape Town when the Japanese attacked Pearl Harbour and Malaya and the brigade was diverted to Singapore. They landed there on 13th January 1942 and were drafted at once into the battle, holding up the Japs for a fortnight. Then, forced to retreat, they burnt their equipment and made their way back to Singapore Island. Finally withdrawing to the perimeter of the town, they carried on until the surrender, by which time Geoffrey had lost a third of his platoon.

By the middle of 1942, a large number of British and Australian prisoners of war had been assembled at Changi, on Singapore Island, and until the Japanese organised them into working parties they led a life of comparative if spartan idleness. Not even their hunger, however, could stop them talking cricket, or even playing it, as soon as the necessary implements were found. Some old, over-oiled bats in the store room, a worn length of matting that was soon patched up, and a few used but usable balls, made the first games possible. Ben Barnett, first choice wicket-keeper with the 1938 Australians, was in the camp, and other well-known names were Len Muncer, of the Green Howards, and Brian Castor, of the Provost Branch. 'It was not long,' writes Ben Barnett, 'before "Test" matches were arranged with our English neighbours.'

One afternoon in August 1942, E. W. 'Jim' Swanton, then a major in the gunners, was walking past the old cricket field at Changi when he saw a game in progress. 'As the bowler ran up to bowl,' he wrote afterwards, 'from a longish run, throwing himself with great energy into the delivery, I thought to myself, "Goodness, I didn't know the Japs had caught Bill Edrich." I can't remember quite how long the illusion persisted, but of course it was Geoffrey. Their figures were extraordinarily similar.'

Geoffrey, of course, was a natural selection for the 'Test' matches, and he seems to have impressed the Australians. 'Even under those conditions,' says Ben Barnett, 'it was obvious that Geoff was a top-class player, and his splendid batting gave a lot of pleasure to the many prisoners who watched those games.' The Japanese, however, had another kind of test waiting for them, of unexampled severity. Before the end of that year, most of the prisoners, and certainly all those fit enough to play cricket, were sent to work on the laying of a railway line over the Siamese hills into Burma – the notorious Thailand Railway. 'Cricket was impossible up there,' says Ben Barnett. 'Work was the order of the day, seven days a week ... Conditions were bad. Food was poor. Geoff, along with all the other POWs who toiled under those inhuman conditions, lost weight and his health suffered.' Dysentery and tropical ulcers were rife, cholera broke out in the worst areas, and hundreds died; but Geoffrey was one of those with the mental and physical equipment to survive. For two years, however, he was recorded among the missing, and nothing was known of his fate.

Brian worked for the first few months of the war on the building of a satellite airfield near Bircham Newton. Then, as had happened so often before, Bill senior's farm was sold over their heads and they had to move. This time help came from a

London banker named John Robarts who used to shoot near-by. 'I've got a home farm where I live in the Buckingham area,' he said. 'I'm not satisfied with the man who's looking after it. Would you consider a move from Norfolk to Buckinghamshire?' 'I've got to do something,' said Bill senior, 'I'll go and have a look at it.' Tilehurst Farm, the home farm, occupied 500 acres of the 3,000-acre estate, and although it was neglected, with a poorly graded herd, Bill senior could see its possibilities. He stayed there until John Robarts died fourteen years later.

Shortly after they moved in, a man named Alec Bell rode up on a horse. 'You play cricket, don't you?' For the next two years, 1940 and 1941, Eric and Brian played for Buckingham. Brian's call-up, deferred until March 1942, then came through and he joined the RAF as a trainee pilot. The receiving centre to which he was ordered to report was Lord's.

Thus for three of the Edrich brothers there was little or no cricket for the next three years. As a gesture towards them, Eric resolved to play no more cricket until the war was over. It was a resolve that, with certain understandable exceptions, he kept.

The only Edrich who was getting any chance to develop his game was the five-year-old John. Like his cousins before him, he was going through the motions on a concrete wicket behind a Norfolk farmhouse. 'My father,' says John, in his book *Runs in the Family*, 'was a useful player, and he devoted all the time he could spare to coaching and encouraging me. He never attempted to convert my natural left-handed tendency, and always insisted I should get behind the ball, which came through truly on the hard surface.' Like Cis a generation back, John's sister Freda often joined in.

Bill got the occasional representative game for the RAF, but his form with bat and ball, against players whose opportunities were often less limited than his, was mediocre. From this period, however, two significant meetings emerged. One was his first encounter with Australian Air Force pilot Keith Miller, in 1944. The other was with the former Northamptonshire and Glamorgan seam bowler Austin Matthews, then a flight lieu-tenant in the RAF. Matthews was one of the greatest exponents

Bill running up to bowl to Don Bradman in the Third Test at Leeds, 1938; *below*, on his way to beating Tom Hayward's record aggregate in the Champion County v. The Rest game at the Oval, 1947

Above, *left,* Geoffrey; *right,* Eric; *below,* Lancashire 1st XI, 1948:
back row, l to r, E. H. Edrich, R. Tattersall, A. Wharton, J. T. Ikin,
G. A. Edrich, A. Barlow; front, W. B. Roberts, C. Washbrook, K.
Cranston, N. D. Howard, R. Pollard, W. Place

The Middlesex Twins,
1947

Below, the 1947 All-Edrich XI: l to r, W.J., W.A., G.A., E.H., B.R.,
Edwin H., Arthur E., George C., George H., Peter G., Harry M.,
Dudley (12th Man)

The Edrich straight drive, by Bill, *left*, and Geoffrey; *below*, the one that got away: Bill beaten for pace by Ray Lindwall in the Second Test at Lord's, 1948

of pitching the ball on the seam; with a high action, he concentrated his skill on making the ball move off the pitch rather than in the air. 'I asked him one day to show me how to do it,' says Bill, 'and he promised he would. But in the rush of wartime postings we never got around to it.'

In 1945, immediately after the surrender of Germany, the first of a series of Victory Test Matches between sides representing England and Australia began at Lord's. Batting for the first four Tests at No. 6, Bill did well enough to hold a place in the side throughout the five matches, and he finished up by topping the batting averages at 47.28. But his two wickets cost him 81 runs each.

The most memorable game of that year, however, was the England *v*. Dominions match in late August at Lord's. In England's first innings Bill, batting No. 8, joined Wally Hammond at 96 for six after Australia had made 307. They put on 177 and restored the balance of the game, and this must count as Bill's best innings of the summer. But despite a hundred in each innings from Hammond, and 109 in the match from Bill, the Dominions won by 45 runs with eight minutes to spare.

Throughout that summer, Geoffrey remained a prisoner of the Japanese, counting himself lucky to be alive. Following the privations of the Thailand-Burma railway, he was sent back to Japan in a convoy of fifteen ships, twelve of which were sunk on the way. It was not until 15th August 1945 that American planes flew over his camp in Honshu Island and dropped food and clothing, and it was another three months before he got back to England via America. Landing at Southampton from the Queen Elizabeth on 5th November, he was at once called upon to report to the Army Welfare Department at the quayside.

It had not been until the summer of 1944 that news had come through that Geoffrey was a prisoner of war. During all that time Olga had been receiving a widow's pension, so the assumption clearly was that her husband was dead. For Olga, with her young son, much water had passed under the bridge. The Army Welfare Officer advised Geoffrey to go back to his parents' home in Buckinghamshire and sort things out from there.

Once again the character and resilience of Geoffrey Edrich was put to the test. With his domestic happiness marred by the war, with his ability to recapture his form as a cricketer open to question, and with his strength and stamina in serious doubt, he faced the task, at the age of twenty-seven, of trying to make a career. Yet cricket was the only thing he knew. It was either that or driving a tractor on the farm.

What he needed above all was the encouragement of those around him, and this, in the Buckinghamshire home of his father, he had in abundance. Hitherto Eric had scarcely considered himself seriously as a first-class cricketer; he felt he wasn't good enough. But now he sensed that Geoffrey needed his comradeship. 'What about it?' he asked Geoffrey soon after he got back. 'What about the first-class game? Is it too late?' Geoffrey's response was immediate. 'What about going together, then?' 'Good idea, Geoff,' said Eric. 'We'll have a go.'

But first Geoffrey had to prove to himself that his sight and reactions were unimpaired, and he and Eric practised with bat and ball on the lawn at Tilehurst Farm, just like old times at Upton and Cantley. When Geoffrey found that he could still middle it, he set about getting himself fit. His legs let him down at first, but during those winter months he slowly began to regain his strength.

In 1945 Eric had played a game or two as a wicket-keeper for Northamptonshire, and he began by ringing them up. They had just re-signed a wicket-keeper named Greenwood who had played for them in 1938–39, and they weren't interested; but when Eric discovered that Greenwood was thirty-seven he cheered up a lot. Perhaps at thirty-one he wasn't too old after all. Hampshire's pre-war interest in Geoffrey, however, had lapsed, and several other counties were tried without success. Eventually, spending a week-end in Norfolk, they called on old friends in Jack Nichols and Michael Falcon.

The advice they got surprised them: try Lancashire. Jack Nichols had once been on the staff at Old Trafford and it was he who first suggested it. But Michael Falcon backed the advice up with sound practical reasons. Lancashire, he believed, would be desperate for players. 'To decide to play in 1946 was one thing,' writes A. W. Ledbrooke in the official history of Lancashire County Cricket, 'to find a team at all worthy of Lancashire's traditions was quite another.' Eddie Paynter, Norman Oldfield and Albert Nutter were going into the Leagues, Hopwood was suffering from ill health, Dick Pollard was still in the Forces, Bill Farrimond was forty-four and Jack Iddon 43. Falcon wrote at once to Major Rupert Howard, the Lancashire secretary, and within a few weeks both Geoffrey and Eric had accepted contracts at £313 for the season, without ever setting foot in Manchester. Both the brothers, as it happened, were known to some of the Lancashire players through playing for Norfolk before the war against Lancashire II, and this may have helped.

Eric's attitude was that he could always go back to farming. So why not have a crack? But Geoffrey knew that there was more to it than that. 'He thought in all the circumstances I ought to have an elder brother around. That was how I read it.'

Bill was demobilised in December 1945 and would of course be returning to Middlesex, but Brian, last of the brothers to enter the Services, was inevitably scheduled to be last out. Having won his RAF wings in Canada, Brian had flown Vultee Vengeances in India before being posted to air-sea rescue work in Ceylon as a warrant-officer pilot, and he faced the prospect of continuing in that role throughout 1946. There was only one way out – to apply for a 'B' class demobilisation to return to agriculture, and this he did; but it precluded him from playing cricket for Kent that summer.

Here was yet another year lost by the Edriches to cricket. And six seasons had passed since Brian's year of initiation with Kent, in only two of which he had had any cricket at all. 'I had nowhere near learnt my trade before the war,' says Brian, 'and I would not have been happy to go straight into county cricket after playing so little. Indeed I doubt if it would have done me any good. I was still only twenty-four, and I felt there was plenty of time.'

Brian, like all his brothers, was philosophical. And as far as Kent were concerned, they fully understood the position, and they gave Brian the occasional Second XI game that season and prepared to welcome him back in 1947.

Thrilled at the prospect of being joined by two of his brothers in the first-class game, Bill drove them up to Manchester on 31st March 1946. 'He was driving an old Humber,' remembers Geoffrey, 'and we had two "flats" on the way. I thought we'd never get there.' They arrived in time for a quick look at the ground before Bill dropped them at their digs 200 yards away off Talbot Road. Next morning, 1st April, they began their new careers. 'But what a day to report!' says Eric. After dismissing his chances of making the grade in first-class cricket all his life, here he was trying his luck with one of the most powerful cricketing counties at the age of thirty-one.

With the qualification rules specially eased, Lancashire had engaged B. P. King, a robust Yorkshireman who had scored four pre-war hundreds for Worcestershire, and T. L. Brierley, a reliable wicket-keeper batsman who had had five pre-war seasons with Glamorgan, in addition to the two Edriches. They were also entering a side in the Minor Counties championship to develop home-grown players, so competition would be keen.

On that first morning at Old Trafford, Geoffrey remembers particularly the friendliness of Eddie Phillipson, the Lancashire all-rounder. 'We were strangers in a strange land,' he says, 'and the whole atmosphere was strange to us too.' But Harry Makepeace, the Lancashire coach, soon put them through their paces. 'Pad up, Geoff,' he said, when the introductions had been made, 'and go down to that net.' Then he switched the bowlers about and studied the result. Dick Pollard, Eddie Phillipson, Len Wilkinson, the leg-spinner, Gordon Garlick, the off-spinner, and the two slow left-armers Eric Price and Bill Roberts, were all permutated and shunted around by Makepeace for the next half-hour. 'That'll do, Geoff,' said Makepeace eventually. And as Geoffrey walked out of the net he called him over. 'The

Lancashire side will be going south on a four-match tour at the end of the month,' he said. 'We'll be playing Cambridge, a Home Counties' side, Oxford, and Gloucestershire at the Wagon Works. You're on the trip.'

'This was just the right thing for me at that time,' admits Geoffrey. He needed a lift, and this gave it to him. 'I think a season in the Seconds would have finished me,' he says. After three weeks' net practice, and a couple of trial games, the party left for Cambridge on Friday 3rd May. Chosen as wicket-keeper, not surprisingly, was the experienced Brierley; but Eric, concerned mainly for his brother, was happy enough to play for the Seconds. 'It was the same sort of cricket as I'd played for Norfolk,' he says, 'and I was getting paid for it.'

Geoffrey got his try-out in the second match, a two-day fixture against the Home Counties at Slough. 'I got about 20,' he remembers, 'and then I was lbw. I hit the ball pretty hard on to the pad and got this bad decision, just when I wanted to do well. And I thought, that's the finish.' But when the side was chosen for the Gloucestershire match he found he was in it.

Gloucestershire had one of the best sides in the country at that time, but despite a century from Hammond they trailed on first innings, and Geoffrey, with knocks of 21 and 48 not out, helped Lancashire to victory, and showed at the same time that he was equally at home against the quickies of Lambert and the spinners of Goddard and Cook.

Three things emerged for Geoffrey from this tour. First he was aware of a subtle change in his temperament. As with many former POWs, he was more highly strung now. Second, he found that the war years had slowed him down, and that his knees, particularly, reacted after a long day in the field. (He was, in fact, still on a 20 per cent disability pension that year.) Thirdly, he could no longer be sure of throwing in first bounce from the ring. He would have to become an in-fielder; and fortunately he found that his reactions near the bat were exceptionally quick. In the Lancashire side as constituted at that time he frequently fielded at slip; but this changed with the arrival of Roy Tattersall a few years later.

69

On the first morning of the Roses match at Sheffield in early June, after only six championship matches, and one 50 (albeit a crucial one against the spin of Roly Jenkins of Worcestershire), Geoffrey was awarded his county cap. He responded with an innings of dour resistance after Yorkshire had declared and Lancashire had lost Washbrook, Ikin and King for 30. There had been a lot of rain, the ball was turning, and Ellis Robinson, the off-spinner, and Arthur Booth, left-arm slow, were taking full advantage. 'Winston Place was at the other end,' says Geoffrey, 'and he was a great chap to bat with. He was such a fine player of the ball leaving the bat, the one that gets the good player out. He came down the wicket and said: "Geoffrey, I think you'll do better down the off-spinner's end. So we'll stay put, twos and fours." In fact we played about eight consecutive maidens. We couldn't get them away – it was a battle for survival. But we eventually put on about 60. It was one of those times when a little help from the other end makes all the difference.'

All this time Eric was keeping wicket and making a few runs for the Seconds; but with Tom Brierley losing concentration behind the wicket, and running into a bad patch with the bat, the chance for Eric to join his brother eventually came in mid-July against Derbyshire. It was unfortunate that in this same match Geoffrey should break a finger while facing Bill Copson; but Eric took his chance with typical volatility, taking four catches and scoring 24. The hair, neatly parted high up, was beginning to thin a little at the front, but the buoyant enthusiasm was there for all to see. Like Bill only five feet six, but thicker-set, he was described by one critic as 'short and rotund, but light on his feet', and by another as 'stout, mirthful and debonair'. In his second match, which was the return Roses fixture, he played another useful knock, dancing down the wicket to Ellis Robinson. 'Edrich took nine runs in an over of Robinson's,' said one report, 'including the now familiar cover drive.' This, in his second match, was praise indeed. 'Bowes returned to the Stretford end to slow up a scoring rate which was becoming positively hectic. His first ball was a long hop and Edrich cut it square and violently to the rails.' How Eric loved the cut! He helped Phil King in a stand of 71 in an hour, then slashed once too often. 'He had a gallivanting off drive,' wrote T. C. F. Prittie, 'and a whimsical way of laughing at his own mistakes.' Here was a refreshing newcomer to the first-class game.

Because of his broken finger, Geoffrey was out of the game for over a month; but the rest, in this his first season of six-days-a-week cricket, did him good, and he came back for the last four matches and did well. 'A brilliant innings by G.A. Edrich,' was how *Wisden* described his 73 against Hampshire, and his 91 against Sussex – the nearest he got that year to a hundred – was made in similar vein, forcing the pace when wickets were falling to make a declaration possible. In these matches he established himself as the Lancashire No. 3, and in 27 innings in the County Championship he made 931 runs at an average of 42, putting him third behind Washbrook and Place for Lancashire. With no big scores to bolster his figures, it was a remarkable performance for a first season. 'Geoffrey Edrich was consistent,' said *Wisden*, 'and, improving steadily, seemed destined for further efficiency.' For all his moments of brilliance, and his ability to suit his game to the conditions, it was his dedicated professionalism that distinguished him from the ruck of county batsmen. *Wisden* also had a good word for Eric. 'E. H. Edrich filled the position behind the stumps with increasing ability as the season advanced.'

There could hardly be a more romantic tale than this story of two contrasting brothers, one turning professional at thirty-one as a gesture of comradeship to his brother and making good, the other picking up the broken threads of his career against all the odds and establishing himself with a leading county side. Lancashire won 15 of their 26 championship matches that year and finished third in the table.

Concurrently with the emergence of the Lancashire Edriches, another Edrich was struggling for a break-through in the south. Bill might well have imagined, after his successful run in the Victory Tests, that he had played himself back into the England side. Not a bit of it. Just as, after the 1938–39 tour of South Africa, the availability of Compton and Hardstaff had combined to squeeze him out of the side, so these same two players displaced him on their return from war service in India.

His omission from the first Test against India he accepted as justified on form alone. He had had a disastrous May, he could do nothing with the ball, and although he ran into form at the beginning of June he failed in the Test Trial. It wasn't until July that he really began to score heavily, and by then the shape of the England side was clearly defined. Hutton, Washbrook, Compton, Hammond, Hardstaff, Gibb, Ikin; that was the batting line-up, and after another Trial, from which Bill was excluded altogether, the same side was chosen for the second of the three Tests. By this time, however, Bill had begun a campaign aimed at forcing his way back into the reckoning.

It wasn't so much the third Test against India that was on his mind. Under pressure from Australia, the MCC had agreed to send out a touring party that winter, playing five Tests. Timing his arrival on the first-class scene badly, Bill had missed the 1936–37 tour, and he couldn't bear the thought of missing this one. His keenness was the greater because of the friendships he had made amongst Australians during the war. Yet, as the names began to be announced, and his was not among them, he could see his chance receding.

On 19th June Middlesex went to play Glamorgan at Swansea, and there Bill met up again with Austin Matthews. Watching him bowl, and seeing how carefully he fingered the ball, Bill took Matthews up on his promise. 'He was interested,' says Bill, 'and at the end of the day we had a long talk. He got a cricket ball and showed me painstakingly what he thought could be done to improve my grip. Somehow Matthews' explanations lighted something up in my mind that had been dark before.'

Bill repaid Matthews' non-partisan kindness by getting three quick wickets next morning; but this was no more than a fluke. He still had to perfect his technique over long hours of bowling. And there was precious little time.

72

No player in the history of the game has put more into his cricket over a short spell than Bill did in the latter part of that 1946 summer. He began July by failing to get runs at Nottingham. Then, against Hampshire, he made 50 and 93 not out. A double failure against Somerset, when Harold Gimblett got 231, was redeemed to some extent by his longest bowl of the season so far, 28 overs, two for 101. Against Essex he made 44 and 111 and picked up three wickets. Then, against Gloucestershire at Lord's, after a duck in the first innings, he came back typically with 127 not out, out of a total of 169, in the second.

No one who saw this innings is likely to forget it. The only other Middlesex man who got more than 6 was Price, who made 23. Such were the conditions that 24 wickets fell on the Saturday, and they were no better when play was resumed on the Monday. It was a real turning sticky, and Goddard, from the pavilion end, and Cook, from the Nursery end, both knew how to use the slope. 'I made up my mind,' says Bill, 'to hit with the spin. Luck was with me, and I got away with it.' But it was much more than luck. It was preposterous. The Tavern was peppered with flying hits that always seemed to bisect the catchers, and Goddard had to accept that he was being murdered on a pitch that was absolutely made for him. 'I've seen better shots than that,' muttered Goddard disgustedly, 'in our Gloucester villages.' 'Go on, Tom,' taunted Bill, 'you keep bowling them, I'll keep hitting them.'

A failure with the bat against Kent followed, but it seems to have inspired him with the ball. 'I desperately wanted to go to Australia,' he recalls, 'and although I was getting plenty of runs by this time, others were making big scores and I knew it wasn't enough. If I'm not good enough as a batsman, I told myself, I must produce good bowling and good fielding.'

Most captains will give a player that little extra exposure if he seems to have a chance of catching the selectors' eye, and Walter Robins was no exception. Bill was getting more and more bowling, and at last he was putting Austin Matthews' teaching into practice. 'I was flinging in the lot to produce something,' says Bill, 'but whereas previously I was slinging and hoping, now I was getting my arm higher, and I found that by cutting down the pace a bit I was moving it off the seam. I still bowled fast for a lot of the time, with out-swingers and the occasional break-back, but the seamers gave me variation, and it's the one that moves late off the pitch that's dangerous.'

The results were beginning to show. Two for 36 and five for 30 against Kent, four for 71 and o for 15 against Sussex, and then, sensationally, seven for 69 against Northamptonshire, including the first six in the order, after making 222 not out! This was on 7th, 8th and 9th August, with the side for the final Test about to be picked; he could not have timed it better. Fourteen players had now been named for Australia, and the last three were due to be chosen that week-end. Swanton, in the *Daily Telegraph*, could see no room for Bill – 'unless his recent bowling successes have translated him into the all-rounder class'. And indeed you could not pick up a newspaper in those weeks without getting the feeling that Bill Edrich was *bowling* himself into the England side.

On Sunday 11th August, the side for the Oval Test was announced, and Bill was in it. On the same day, the touring party was completed by the addition of Laurie Fishlock, Jim Langridge, and – the last man to be named – Bill Edrich.

At the end of that 1946 season, Eric got a telegram inviting him to keep wicket at Scarborough for the North against the South. The game had a special sense of occasion as it was Maurice Leyland's last match. Brian Sellers won the toss for the North, and he and Eric were the most successful batsmen, Sellers making 56 and Eric, from No. 8, 53 not out. Maurice Leyland, too, pleased the crowd by making 31 – and runs were not given away in the Scarborough Festival in those days. But what impressed Eric most was the briefing Sellers gave them before they went into the field. Wyatt doesn't like them here, Wilcox (the other opener) doesn't like them there, this one doesn't like them quick round his ears, pitch them up to this one, don't pitch them up to Freddie Brown or Walter Robins – he went right through the batting order, picking out individual weaknesses and strengths. Eric believed that Sellers' shrewd diagnoses played a large part in the North's victory by 130 runs, and he rated Sellers the best captain he had ever played under.

One could not have four sons playing or about to play in county cricket, even in those days, without attracting the attention of the media, and Edith Edrich, in an article published in a Norfolk paper, was prevailed upon to give her recipe for success. 'The boys were brought up on good plain food,' she said. 'Porridge for breakfast with bacon and egg (when old enough). For lunch, Yorkshire pudding, gravy, and plenty of vegetables, milk puddings and suet pudding with golden syrup in winter, and lots of fruit, fresh or in puddings in summer, with cream only occasionally. For tea they had home-made bread and home-made butter and lots of salad foods with the Norfolk shortcake. Supper was often ceral with sugar and plenty of milk. They always had at least twelve hours sleep a night.

'After the quaint little farmhouse at Lingwood, we lived in a lovely old Manor House at Cantley. That was where our boys learned to "hold their bats straight and play down the line of the ball". To their father must go all the credit for teaching them their cricket. He was never tired of playing cricket with them. They loved the game and I used to give them "just a few more minutes" when bedtime came.

'The boys were not at all pleased at first when our daughter Ena was born. "She won't be any good – she won't be able to play cricket," they said.' The family photo album, however, contains a number of pictures which prove that she did.

By the time Eric was playing at Scarborough in September 1946, Bill had already sailed with the MCC party for Australia. He had been appointed senior professional, and Hammond invited him to join himself and the vice-captain, Norman Yardley, on the selection committee. But he still had to make sure of his place in the England team. And that, judging from the early matches, seemed unlikely. There had been much more rain than normal, and conditions were unusually favourable to spin. Bill

had his chances, but he failed. As a batsman he had not acclimatised himself to Australian conditions, which seemed far
different from what he'd been told, and although he picked up
the occasional wicket he could rarely move the ball off the
seam. He was in the side for the final match before the first
Test against Queensland, but by this time Paul Gibb had been
groomed for the No. 3 spot and Bill batted No. 7.

In the match against an Australian XI a fortnight earlier,
the English batsmen, Bill included, had been mesmerised by
the leg spin and googlies of Colin McCool. Now, against
Queensland, they had to face him again. After Queensland
had made 400, Hutton, Washbrook, Gibb and Hammond all
fell to McCool, while Ian Johnson, the off-spinner, got Compton
and Ikin. Then Bill, totally unawed by McCool, began col-
lecting runs in his most enterprising manner. 'The wicket was
taking spin,' wrote one Australian commentator, 'but he showed
his less intrepid companions just how McCool should be
handled.' While C. B. Fry was sending telegrams urging the
English batsmen to stay in their creases, Bill was moving yards
down the wicket in the Hendren manner, and his 64 not out
pulled the game round. Promoted by Hammond in the second
innings to No. 3, much as he had been promoted in 1939 in
Durban, he responded with another fine innings of 71 when
defeat looked probable.

So to the first Test, and the famous incident of the Ikin
catch when Bradman was 28. Surviving the appeal, at a point
when his whole Test future was in the balance, the Don went
on to make 187 before Bill bowled him on the second morning.
The Australians made 645 (Bill three for 107), and then an
overnight thunderstorm killed any chance England had of sav-
ing the game. Nevertheless they fought valiantly. 'Edrich was
struck repeatedly,' wrote Norman Preston, 'and when Hammond
came in nearly every ball from Lindwall rose head high. When
taken at first slip immediately after lunch, Edrich had withstood
the bowling for one and three-quarter hours. He scored only
16, but his was one of the most skilful batting displays I have
ever seen.'

76

Alan Kippax and Australian writer Clif Cary paid similar tributes. 'He suffered more than forty body blows,' wrote Cary, 'with a nonchalant contempt for danger and seemed content to be battered black and blue rather than lose his wicket.' Shades of Close versus Hall seventeen years later! Bill had quickly appreciated that on this sort of Australian gluepot anything short of a half-volley reared so sharply that it went over the top, and by disciplining himself he kept his bat out of the way.

The second Test, at Sydney, although England lost it, was unquestionably Bill's match. After top-scoring in the first innings with 71, he took the first three Australian wickets to fall. Bradman and Barnes then made double centuries; but when England batted again, Bill led the fight to stave off defeat and top-scored, this time with 119 – his first century against Australia. 'He played the spinners with confident assurance,' was one comment, 'and never once did he shrink from the many bumpers that went his way.'

For Bill, these two innings were the final vindication. 'I was no longer worried,' he wrote, 'by the anxiety to prove, before it was too late, that I deserved my place in the side.'

In the third Test, at Melbourne, he was to prove a good deal more. Australia batted first, and within half an hour Bill was off the field and quite conceivably out of the match. He was fielding close up at short leg to Doug Wright, looking for a catch from the googly, when Wright dropped one short and Barnes pulled it with terrific force. 'I never saw it at all after it left the bat,' says Bill, and he collapsed with pain as the ball struck the inside of his knee. A huge lump appeared almost at once on the knee, and when he tried to stand he couldn't put his weight on it. He stayed for an over or so, then was persuaded to go off. When Voce left the field soon after lunch with a pulled muscle, England's situation looked hopeless; but Bedser and Wright bowled magnificently, Yardley directed his medium-paced leg theory with wonderful accuracy, and at close of play Australia were 255 for six.

To everyone's astonishment, Bill not only appeared on the

field next morning, but bowled the first over, although he was still slightly lame. And with his first ball he got Tallon caught behind the wicket. McCool completed a punishing century, but Bill took three of the last four wickets for 50 runs, all caught from snicks around the off stump.

Even now there was no rest for that injured knee. Hutton was beaten by Lindwall almost at once, and Bill joined Washbrook with two-and-a-half hours left for play. At the close England were 147 for one, with Bill, very much the senior partner, 85 not out.

Tragedy was to come next morning. With his score at 89, Bill played a ball from Lindwall hard on to his pad. 'How's that?' asked Lindwall. 'Out,' said the umpire. They must have been the only two men on the ground who didn't hear the sound of bat on ball. But Bill had to go. Soon afterwards, Compton was lbw padding up to Toshack, Hammond, losing concentration, gave his wicket away, and once more England were in trouble. 'This is not a Test Match,' wrote E. M. Wellings in disgust, and even the Australians agreed that the umpiring went against England in this series.

There is no doubt that Bill's batting in these first three Tests had put heart into the others and encouraged them to believe in themselves, and now, in their second innings, they batted well enough to escape defeat. But the extent to which Bill carried the batting up to this stage is underlined by the scores of Hutton, Compton and Hammond, rightly regarded as England's leading batsmen. Hutton made 7, 0, 39, 2 and 40. Compton made 17, 15, 5, 54, 11 and 14. And Hammond's scores were 32 and 23 (at Brisbane, both magnificent efforts), 1 and 37, and 9 and 26.

At Melbourne in the third Test, Washbrook and Yardley joined Bill amongst the run-getters. In the fourth it was the turn of Hutton and Compton. Despite the bowling of persistent bumpers from Lindwall and Miller, Hutton and Washbrook put on over a hundred in each innings, and Compton got two separate hundreds. But the match petered out into a draw.

Despite his abundant energy and stamina, and his amazing

powers of recovery, there is no doubt that by this stage of the tour Bill was tired. 'Sometimes his utter weariness was so apparent that he looked as if he was at dropping point,' wrote Clif Cary. 'Always, however, he was ready for an extra effort when Hammond wanted him. Never once did he fail to throw all he had into his batting, bowling or fielding.' But to some degree, at least, his batting suffered.

In the final Test, Washbrook was bowled by Lindwall in the first over, and Bill joined Hutton to face a barrage of bumpers from Lindwall and Miller. Yet they added 150 in the highest English partnership of the series. England actually got a first-innings lead; but McCool's flighted spin turned the game. 'Even Edrich,' said *Wisden* revealingly, 'was greatly troubled by McCool.' He got to 24 before missing a leg break as he went down the wicket, to be stumped by Tallon. Even then, only Compton (76) made more runs.

Since that gluepot at Brisbane, Bill had scored 71 and 119, 89 and 13, 17 and 46, and 60 and 24, and his average for the series was 46. Hit total of 462 was the highest England aggregate of the series, and only Bradman and Morris scored more. In addition he bowled 115 eight-ball overs and took 9 wickets, and with Bedser, Wright and Yardley he was one of Hammond's four main bowlers. His average of 53 runs per wicket sounds expensive until one looks at the averages of the other three – Yardley 37, Wright 43, Bedser 54.

As for temperament, he had silenced for all time all those who had questioned it. Indeed it was the Test Matches where he excelled – as everyone who really knew him would have expected. 'I think,' concluded Norman Preston in *Wisden*, 'that he became the best man in the side.'

Soon after the Australian tour started, Bill received a letter offering him a chance of a commercial career if he turned amateur, and when he found on his return that his prospective employers were keen for him to continue with his cricket, and that the Middlesex committee were agreeable, he accepted. He thus faced the 1947 season with his security assured, and this may have been a factor in his uninhibited batting that year. But there were other factors too. After all the years of rationing, everyone who had gone to Australia had built up his strength and fitness, while Bill also came back morally fortified and at the top of his form. 'I was thirty-one,' he says, 'and I suppose I was at my peak. It was such a wonderful summer, too – one always felt in form. And after a winter of Lindwall and Miller, things were a trifle easier ... And of course I was batting so much with Denis. You couldn't remain passive when he was at the other end. If he hit three fours in an over, you could hardly play out a maiden. You had to try and match him. I never did, but I certainly tried. We helped each other, though, and between us we didn't give the bowlers much hope.'

Here Bill is being both modest and forgetful. The truth is that it was Denis who was trying to match Bill for most of that astonishing summer.

In his first innings for Middlesex as an amateur, Bill made 102, then took four wickets for five runs next morning and 3 for 47 in the second innings; yet Somerset won a marvellous match by one wicket, and the Middlesex players lined up and cheered their last pair into the pavilion. In the next match, against Gloucestershire, Bill and Denis made only 62 between them, but Gloucester failed twice against the Middlesex opening bowlers (Gray 7 for 51, Bill 8 for 54), and Bill was reliably reported to have 'bowled very fast'. Against Warwickshire he got 225, then it was Denis who took over against Worcestershire with 88 not out and 112. They both got hundreds off Sussex, and when the Test Matches against South Africa came along they were irresistible. Denis reached his 1,000 runs in his seventeenth innings on 10th June, and Bill, who had missed the early MCC matches, reached the target ten days later in three fewer innings. He then overhauled Denis and within the next month won a fantastic race to be first to 2,000.

The orgies of run-getting in which Bill and Denis were concerned seemed never-ending; but perhaps the most fantastic match of all was at Leicester in mid-July, when Bill, captaining Middlesex for the first time in the absence of Robins and

Mann, made what seemed the cardinal error of putting the opposition in. Leicestershire made 309; but Middlesex, batting in a kind of frenzy, replied with 637 for four. After Bill had put on 159 with Jack Robertson, he and Denis added another 277 in two hours ten minutes, and between lunch and tea on the second day Middlesex scored 310. Bill made 257, Denis 151. Undismayed by all this, Leicestershire improved on their first innings performance and with eighty minutes to go on the last day looked absolutely safe. Seventeen runs in front, they still had six wickets to fall.

'We simply *had* to win this match to keep in the hunt for the championship,' says Bill, 'and if we lost our chance because of an error of captaincy I knew I should never forgive myself.' Because of this, Bill adopted tactics which he had often seen Robins use but which were utterly foreign to his nature. He tried *talking* the batsmen out. 'Go on,' he told them, 'have a go. Liven it up a bit. You can't lose now.' And one by one, during the next 35 minutes, they obliged him. When at last they were all out for 393, Middlesex wanted 66 in 25 minutes.

'Come on, Denis,' said Bill. He arranged to have two batsmen with their pads on waiting 'in the wings' behind a sight-screen, and he deployed the others round the perimeter of the field to get the ball back quickly. The runs were made in seven overs with four minutes to spare.

Rather more typical was the game against Essex at Lord's the following week. Batting first, Middlesex made 389 for seven in four hours ten minutes before Robins declared. They then dismissed Essex for 350, got 356 for five in two hours fifty minutes, and set Essex 396 to win. In the finish the men who stood between Middlesex and victory were wicket-keeper Wade and a young Cambridge undergraduate named Trevor Bailey. Despite having six stitches in a hand split while fielding, the barnacle-to-be stuck it out while 49 runs were added for the last wicket before inexplicably getting himself stumped off Robins.

In the next few weeks Bill matched and indeed eclipsed everything Compton could do to catch him up. His was the name at the top of the averages, not Compton's, and against South Africa he was not only top of the batting but England's leading wicket-taker. A feature article about him in *Picture Post* by E. M. Wellings was headlined 'Cricket's Best All-Rounder', while Neville Cardus, watching his 191 in the Third Test at Old Trafford, wrote playfully: 'It is clear that the time has come when something needs to be done, legally if possible, about Edrich.' In those days of ration books his suggestion was that 'it might be fair and proper to put him on a run ration'. Bill's average in all matches at this point was 101.

By the beginning of August, Bill had made 2,358 runs to Compton's 2,071, average 107 against 76, and he seemed certain to be first to 3,000. But throughout that long, hot summer Middlesex, under the dynamic leadership of Robins, were chasing the championship, and Bill was opening the bowling with Laurie Gray as the spearhead of the attack. Robins did not spare him, and he did not spare himself. And in the first week of August, with the championship in the balance, Middlesex hit trouble when Kent ran up a huge total on the first day of the fixture at Canterbury. Late that evening, striving for that extra yard of pace that would shift the tail-enders, Bill tore the muscles under his right shoulder and had to go off the field. 'I doubt whether he will bowl another over in this match,' wrote Jim Swanton in the *Daily Telegraph*. 'If he bats today he will do so under grave difficulties.' Bill certainly couldn't bowl, but with the discipline of which he was capable he restricted his shots in the second innings and made 130.

Brian was not in the Kent side that day, but the brothers met that evening in the hotel where Bill was staying. 'Will you be out of the Oval Test?' Brian asked him. 'It may not be a bad thing if I am,' joked Bill, 'I can help Middlesex win the championship.'

When he got back to London the shoulder had stiffened up so badly that he could hardly move his arm. Yet he was determined to play against Surrey at the Oval next day. He went to see Bill Tucker, the orthopaedic specialist who later operated on Compton's knee. 'You've torn the tendons off the bone,' said Tucker. 'It's going to take some little time to get them right.' 'How am I going to play?' asked Bill. 'Well,' said Tucker, 'I can inject it, and do what I can to repair it, so that it starts to heal. But if you're insistent on playing tomorrow, I'll have to restrict your movement.'

Tucker strapped the shoulder up in such a way that the arm couldn't be lifted above a certain point and the muscles were protected. 'Leave that strapping as it is,' said Tucker, 'and try it out and see if you can bat. You certainly can't bowl or throw.'

Next morning Bill persuaded Robins that he was fit enough to play, and at the end of the day the score-book read: Middlesex 537 for two, Brown 98, Robertson 127, Edrich 157 not out, Compton 137 not out. The final Test was due to be played on the following Saturday, and A. J. Holmes, chairman of selectors, was on the phone to Bill that Sunday morning. 'I see you got some runs yesterday. How are you?' When Bill admitted that he could neither bowl nor throw, that he could only bat in a restricted way, and that he couldn't reach out for any ball going away from him to his right, Holmes decided that he must be left out.

Unfortunately, however, that unguarded remark to Brian at Canterbury had been overheard, and Swanton, in his Monday morning commentary, referred to 'the case of Edrich ... he says he cannot bowl or throw, and indeed bats under limitations, though two hundreds in three days might suggest his resource is well equal to the handicap. Equally undeniable, and also natural, is his keen wish to try to help his county while the Test is in progress. I confess I would have opposed very strongly a precedent which made selection for England dependent on fixtures in the championship.'

Carefully phrased as this comment was, there were others besides Bill who read into it a more personal criticism than perhaps was meant. When Bill ran into Swanton later that day his attention had already been drawn to it. 'I can tell you this, Jim,' he said, in his quiet, undemonstrative way, 'if that inference is not withdrawn, I shall sue.'

Swanton duly amended his notice. The version given to him,

he said, had not been a true one. 'It is clearly due to him [Edrich] that this be made known.'

Bill did not bowl again that season, depriving him of the chance of emulating Jim Parks senior's feat of 3,000 runs and 100 wickets in a season. And even more disappointing, his batting, after those two remarkable innings in adversity against Kent and Surrey, fell away. He did not miss a match, and he went to the wicket another eighteen times before the final game of the season, but in that time he did not score a single century. His aggregate for those eighteen innings was 570, average 31. Meanwhile Denis was romping ahead, and in that final month he scored 1,152 runs and on 9th September passed Tom Hayward's record aggregate of 3,518. Denis, too, was not completely free from injury, as his knee was already troubling him; but it does seem that but for his shoulder injury Bill must have exceeded the 4,000 mark. Even as it was, Denis only beat him to 3,000 by five days.

When the final game, Champion County v. The Rest at the Oval, came to be played, Compton had beaten all conceivable records. But for Bill, the personal disappointments of the past month had left him 172 runs short of Tom Hayward's total. Now he had one match, possibly only one innings, to make it.

Saturday 13th September began as a typical autumn day, a day for umbrellas and mackintoshes, and scudding clouds were darkening the Oval as Robins won the toss. With a small wet patch outside the off stump at the Vauxhall end, this proved something of an embarrassment, and Middlesex were soon 53 for three. But at that point Compton, delayed by a visit to Bill Tucker, joined Bill.

It had become a question of digging the side out of trouble, and throughout that dull morning Bill set his sights no higher than that. At lunch, when the score was 105 for 3, he was 39 not out after nearly two hours at the crease. Compton had batted an hour for 19.

The atmosphere remained strange and unreal, quite unlike anything else since early that year. There were even interruptions for rain, and it wasn't until the Edrich-Compton stand reached a hundred that the crowd came to life. 'Up to that point,' said *The Times*, 'it had sat silently, almost sadly, watching summer and its game drain away.'

Suddenly Bill hit 17 off one over from Goddard; and then Compton, going down the wicket to the same bowler, fell in a heap as his knee gave way. Miraculously he somehow contrived to middle the ball as he fell, sending it humming to the leg boundary; but immediately afterwards he had to retire. Bill, however, went on to his century, and at the close Middlesex were 232 for three, Edrich 113 not out.

By Monday morning the wicket was a beauty, and Bill set his sights firmly on Hayward's record. When Robins was caught off Goddard, Compton returned, and fittingly it was in his company, at a quarter past one, that Bill ran the single that put his aggregate beyond Hayward's. When he was finally stumped – off Goddard – he had made 180.

Compton finished up with 246; but Bill's innings must surely rank as one of the more remarkable of that run-happy summer.

The Rest of England, after following on, just about managed to make Middlesex bat again. Bill had taken his last possible chance.

Brian had rejoined the Kent staff at the beginning of 1947, expecting to play some colts and club and ground cricket, get a few games for the Seconds, and put in plenty of practice. But the reality was different. 'Put your pads on, Brian,' he was told soon after he arrived. 'You're going in the nets.' Doug Wright, Ray Dovey and Fred Ridgway bowled at him, with the committee watching, and when the session was over he was told: 'You're playing on Saturday.' 'I had nowhere near learnt my trade,' says Brian, 'but now I was thrown in at the deep end – and that proved to be Bill Copson. The first ball I faced in first-class cricket was from him.

'He struck me on the pad and appealed loudly, glared at me down the wicket when his appeal was turned down, and growled at me at the end of the over: "That was plumb." I managed to make 24, and I was pleased with that; but then the struggle started.'

Lancashire's first match in the County Championship that year happened to be against Kent, at Old Trafford, and all three of Bill's brothers were on view. Kent batted first and were all out for 102; Brian got a duck, bowled Pollard. Lancashire replied with 180, and Kent were in deep trouble in their second innings when Brian came in on a 'pair'.

What were the feelings of the brothers when they played against each other? 'When we played Middlesex,' says Geoffrey, 'we always wanted to get Bill out, and he certainly did his best to get us out. But when we were playing Kent we wanted Brian to get runs. I suppose that was natural.'

With Eric keeping wicket and Geoffrey in the gully, they were unbearably close to the action. And Dick Pollard, who had bowled Brian in the first innings, had scented blood. Brian struggled for over after over as Pollard gave nothing away, and for Eric and Geoffrey it was agony. 'Push one and run,' they urged, 'we won't run you out.' Eventually they could stand it no longer. 'For God's sake, Brian,' they hissed as they crossed between overs, 'get off the bloody mark!' Eventually he did so, with a snicked four and a three, then got out at the other end. Lancashire won comfortably by eight wickets.

Lancashire's fourth home match that year was against Surrey, and it was a significant one for both the northern Edriches. Reluctant to take the risk of putting Surrey in on a pitch affected by rain, Ken Cranston, the new Lancashire skipper, elected to bat. Lancashire were put out for 180, and only Geoffrey among the batsmen reached 20. Surrey made 435, but then a masterly 251 from Washbrook, helped in a stand of 143 by Geoffrey, saved Lancashire from defeat. Eric, too, helped in the rearguard action, but he had sustained cracked ribs while keeping wicket, and Brierley came in for the next two matches. In the second of them he made his first century for Lancashire and thus barred the way for Eric's return. When Brierley was supplanted in turn by a newly-signed wicket-keeper from Bolton in the thirty-one-year-old Alf Barlow, who kept his place for the rest of the season, Eric's future seemed in doubt.

Geoffrey's first championship hundred came at Blackpool in June, after Lancashire had been put in to bat. From then on he was wonderfully consistent, scarcely ever failing to play at least one important innings per match. In many ways the season belonged to the opening pair, Washbrook and Place, who scored 16 centuries between them; but it was usually after a bad start that Geoffrey made his best scores. In his second century that season, 132 against Essex at Clacton, he put on 270 with Place after Washbrook and Ikin had gone cheaply, in what *Wisden* described as 'a lively exhibition of enterprising play'. Lancashire won by an innings.

Taking stock at the end of that season, Geoffrey could feel that he was now firmly established in the first-class game. He stood 16th in the first-class averages in that year of heavy scoring with an average of 44, and he had developed a wider range of stroke. Such, unfortunately, could not be said of Eric or Brian. Eric played in only four championship matches and clearly had to regard himself as second or third choice behind the wicket, while for Brian it had been a discouraging season.

'They pushed me in too soon,' he thinks. 'I should have had at least half a season in the nets before I went into the side. My technique wasn't good, partly because I had missed much of the net practice and coaching that I would normally have had in my teens. I'd even forgotten much of what I'd learnt before the war. I was basically a natural player, not a "made" player at all, and I can see now that I was nowhere near ready for the first-class game.

'I was getting out a lot lbw through hitting across the line, and if I had a lad doing this at school today I'd get him out of it in a month. But the men who were coaching Kent then didn't do this. Perhaps it was my fault; perhaps after my years in the RAF I wasn't very receptive. I don't know. It's easy to blame the war, but the time to learn is in one's teens.'

Brian certainly couldn't complain at the chances he was given, but in 17 first-class knocks he averaged less than 10. He did better with the bat for the Seconds, but for neither side did he do much with the ball.

That winter MCC sent a side to tour the West Indies, but Bill, invited on an expenses-only basis, declined on business grounds. 'Place and Edrich (Geoffrey), it would seem, are likely to be considered for the tour,' wrote Alf Clarke in the *Manchester Evening Chronicle*; and his forecast in the same article that Ken Cranston might also be invited, probably as vice-captain, suggests that he was not ill-informed, since Cranston was in fact chosen in that capacity. Place too was duly selected, but not Geoffrey. 'He tells me he is not too keen,' wrote Clarke. 'He spent so many years in a Japanese prisoner-of-war camp that England has a stronger appeal at the moment.' And here again he had inside information. Geoffrey and Olga had been reunited that year, and they had rediscovered all their early married happiness and were planning to reinforce their family; it was certainly not an opportune time for them to part again. Yet Geoffrey at this time was a more complete player than some who went on the tour. This was apparent not so much from the big scores as from the more modest ones in adversity; two such innings, of 31 and 25, were played against Yorkshire at Sheffield that summer. 'Edrich had failed to save the follow-on by only one run,' was one comment on his 31, 'in an innings of remarkable vigilance and calm.'

All else in 1948 was overshadowed by Bradman's farewell tour. The side he brought has been reckoned to be the greatest ever to come from Australia; but it is a fact that the special regulations governing the availability of the new ball gave his attack a tremendous advantage. Three great bowlers, Lindwall, Miller and Johnston, shared the new ball, and then Bradman shut the game up until, after a mere 55 overs, the next new ball became due. This of course was Compton's series, 562 runs at an average of 62, but Hutton, Washbrook and Bill Edrich, after a bad start, came out of a difficult series with credit.

After the first two Tests had been lost by huge margins,

the cry went out for scalps. Washbrook's place was in doubt, and so was Bill's, but it was Hutton who was dropped, on the basis of a supposed failure of nerve at Lord's. As for scalps, it was Compton's that suffered when he failed to get hold of a Lindwall bumper at Old Trafford. 'With Edrich seemingly afraid to play his strokes in a determined effort to redeem previous low scores and Compton not settled down, Lindwall began a number of bouncers one of which led to an accident to Compton,' said *Wisden*. Getting a top edge to a no-ball, he was hit on the forehead and staggered off.

The reference to Bill is typical of the atmosphere in which the England side was selected, and it seems incredible in retrospect that the problems facing England's four premier batsmen of the period were not better appreciated. Bill's batting in this innings was certainly laboured, but by staying three hours ten minutes for 32 he held the fort while Compton rested. Compton came back to play the innings of his life, England totalled 363, and with Barnes absent hurt through a crippling blow received while fielding, Australia were dismissed for 221.

Facing the prospect of defeat, Lindwall and Miller flung themselves into the attack with unparalleled virulence in an effort to recover lost ground. Emmett was out at once, and Bill joined Washbrook to face probably the most violent assault ever mounted by these two bowlers. In an atmosphere that approached that of the 'bodyline' series, with the crowd angered by a succession of bumpers from Miller, Bill was the safer of the two. But neither man would give way, and in a stand of 124 they silenced all their critics. When they had put England into a winning position, however, the weather intervened.

Had England played Jack Young in the fourth Test at Leeds they must have won it; the story of that final day, when Australia scored 404 for three to win the match, still makes Englishmen toss in their sleep. But Bill, with 111 and 54, had his best match of the series.

So to the disasters of the Oval, where only Hutton distinguished himself. 'I felt afterwards that we should have put them in,' says Bill. 'The sky was overcast and conditions were right for good controlled swing bowling. Lindwall was pitching about middle stump and carrying on to hit the off or there-abouts, and of course he bowled magnificently.' England were all out for 52 (Lindwall six for 20), and they never got back into the game.

In the County Championship that year Bill made six hundreds and averaged 60, and he generally managed to match Compton run for run and shot for shot. One match where he didn't, though, was against Somerset at Lord's in mid-May. They put on 424 together, of which Compton's share was 252; and of 209 added in seventy minutes after tea Compton made 139. 'There was a chap called Miles Coope playing for Somerset,' says Bill, 'and if you look at his bowling analysis you'll find he took o for 60.' (It was o for 61.) 'The wicket was pitched on the Grand Stand side of the ground, and Coope bowled from the Nursery end. Denis kept hitting him on to the Grand Stand balcony, but he kept the party to himself. I didn't get up that end for a single ball.'

'Where do you bowl to them?' asked Arthur Wellard des-pairingly, after changing from seam to off-spin and getting much the same treatment. He never found out the answer, not that day anyway, finishing with o for 158.

Another bowler who suffered nightmares against them was Eric Hollies, of Warwickshire. 'Eric was a good flighter of the ball,' says Bill, 'but he didn't spin it very much, and Denis and I could read his googly without any trouble.' They put on 121 against him that year in 80 minutes. 'When he realised we'd rumbled him,' says Bill, 'he used to give up bowling leg-breaks altogether and just bowl off-spin to keep it tight.' Later, when they were out, he would revert to his normal style and clean up the tail.

In 1948 the Edrich of the year, though, was undoubtedly Eric. Coming into the Lancashire side as a batsman against Warwickshire at Old Trafford on 12th May, with Alf Barlow keeping wicket, he was surprised when Cranston put him in No. 5. 'It was my first chance as a batsman, and my first time up the order,' says Eric, 'and I thought, I've got to grab it.' And grab it he did. 'Hollies was bowling when I got in,' he says, 'and I had to play his leg-spinners and googlies from the start. I could pick him fairly well, being a wicket-keeper, but I played him mostly off the pitch.' 'Eric,' said one writer, 'was in warlike mood,' and he made a splendid 106 not out in 155 minutes. 'Several of his late cuts were beautifully done, and he was the first batsman not afraid to hit the slow bowlers back over their heads into an unguarded deep.' Here was another Edrich headache for Hollies. 'Short balls were slashed or hooked, and when he did misjudge a ball and was beaten he never allowed the matter to distress him.' All this was typical Eric. Although out first thing next morning, he had made his first hundred for the county, 'with many cultured strokes', according to *Wisden*. 'If he'd gone to Lord's when Bill did,' believes Geoffrey, 'there wouldn't have been much between them.' He played very straight and had all the shots, and like all the Edriches he was a great 'leaver' when the ball turned; he had the ability to get right back, judge the width of his stumps, and leave the ball late.

The next match, starting on Whit-Saturday, was against Yorkshire at Leeds, and Eric, again batting No. 5, joined Washbrook on the first morning at 57 for three. Overshadowed by Washbrook, with whom he put on 170, he was still there at close of play with 76 not out. And fortunately his highly distinctive style and manner at the wicket were caught that day for posterity by Denys Rowbotham of the *Guardian*. If he could not bring to the game the bloom of a Washbrook, said Rowbotham, he brought the next best thing, his own unalloyed joy and delight. 'Edrich is a merry, unselfconscious humorist, he loves every ball that is bowled to him and grins happily at every crack of his bat on it. He plays too far away from his body for a good batsman, but he defends with an intensive crouched watchfulness, hits with a West Countryman's relish and lustiness, and has a delayed flourish of the bat in his follow-through that is strikingly his own; it is hardly integral to his shots and one day he may knock off his own head with it, but it must give him, as it certainly does the spectator, the impression that he has generously played two strokes to each ball.'

A hundred against Yorkshire! Could he do it? That was the burden of his thoughts during that Whitsun week-end. On the Monday morning he was nervous for the first time, and when he got into the nineties he repeated to himself the old (supposedly apocryphal) quotation: 'I'll get them in singles.' Painstakingly, but with the Yorkshire crowd urging him on in spite of themselves, the century was reached. 'Then Edrich threw all caution to the winds and hit wildly and exultantly as any schoolboy, driving Wardle for 4 and 6 and treating Smailes to the same cheerful disrespect ... The Yorkshire crowd cheered him loudly; he had established himself as a character and a lovable cricketer.'

In the next match, against Glamorgan at Old Trafford, Eric set his eye on another hundred. But Lancashire, batting second, lost three batsmen quickly at the end of the first day and sent in first one and then another night watchman, so that Eric didn't go in until No. 8. But Ikin was going well at the other end, and Wharton was still to come, so Eric felt he still had a chance. He had made 18 when he slipped turning for a second run, Ikin didn't notice it, and Eric was run out. When he reached the pavilion he was met in the doorway by Harry Makepeace. 'Let's have a look at your studs.' He had forgotten to check them, and had let them wear right down.

Otherwise he could do nothing wrong in that first month of the season. Back at No. 5, he made 63 against Hampshire, accelerating as the time approached for a declaration, and running a single more than once to the wicket-keeper standing back. Then he was picked as wicket-keeper against the Australians.

After the first day had been lost through rain, Cranston put the Australians in, and the two left-arm slow bowlers Bill Roberts and Malcolm Hilton caused a collapse. Bradman was bowled for 11 by the seventeen-year-old Hilton, which naturally made the headlines (actually he played on), and the whole side were out for 204. Geoffrey then top-scored with 55 out of Lancashire's 182, and when the Australians went in a second time, Bradman was again bothered by Hilton. Then, as though determined to show who was master, he gave Hilton the charge. Twice he sent him to the ropes, but the third time Hilton saw him coming and dropped the ball a bit shorter. It turned a little, beat Bradman, and went through at bail height just outside the off stump.

Eric may not have been a great wicket-keeper, but in a modest way he was, like Bradman himself, something of a showman. 'Rickie didn't take the bails off straight away,' says Geoffrey. 'He waited for the great man to turn, see his wicket still intact, and try to scramble back. Then he quietly removed a bail. It must have been torture for Bradman, but if he'd taken them off straight away he'd have missed half the fun.'

A hundred against Yorkshire, to play against the Australians, and then to stump Bradman! It was beyond Eric's wildest dreams. But he says: 'Anybody could have stumped him. I was lucky enough to be behind the wicket.' Did he deliberately tantalise Bradman by delaying for a second or so, as Geoffrey suggests? His answer has a suspicion of tongue-in-cheek. 'I was just a bit slow getting them off.'

The next match, against Middlesex at Lord's, once again showed Eric at his best. After stumping Harry Sharp off Roberts, he committed perhaps the most unbrotherly offence of all by stumping Bill off Hilton. Because of rain the game hadn't started until four o'clock on the second day, but by the last afternoon it had developed into a tense battle for first innings lead, then worth four points. (A win counted twelve.)

Middlesex were all out for 192, leaving Lancashire just over three hours to make the runs. When the second wicket fell, to a Bill Edrich break-back, 98 were wanted in 65 minutes.

The not out batsman was Geoffrey, and No. 4 would normally have been Ikin. But Cranston conceived the idea of sending Eric in next. With Bill bowling flat out from the pavilion end, Cranston saw the possibilities of pitting brother against brother in a bitter/sweet fraternal onslaught. There would have been no holds barred anyway, but after that stumping off Hilton, the main target for the bouncers was bound to be Eric. Fortunately

Eric could hook. 'They stole runs with placed shots at first,' wrote one correspondent. 'Then they began to use their feet and take risks. Both batsmen pulled or hooked anything short and glanced Young to fine leg – the one unguarded place on the field – with repeated glee and maliciousness.' *The Times* summed it up : 'These two Edriches were in no mood to be tamed, and so won for Lancashire a first-innings match which must have been a joy for any one-day club cricketer to watch.' Instant cricket was casting its shadows before.

In the next home match, Eric was awarded his county cap. But despite all these spectacular successes, his position in the Lancashire side seems never to have been altogether secure. It was natural, once he succeeded as a batsman, that the committee should try to save a place in the side by appointing him wicket-keeper as well. But once he was behind the stumps he found it harder to hold his position at No. 5, especially when Cranston, Wharton and Nigel Howard started to make runs. Batting at No. 8, he found runs harder to get, while considered purely as a wicket-keeper he was under pressure from Brierley, Barlow and a new man named Wilson. Then, early in July, standing up to Cranston at Taunton, he bruised a hand so badly that Brierley had to take over in the second innings, and soon afterwards he lost his place in the side.

Nevertheless, playing in 15 of the 26 championship matches, he scored 501 runs, including the two hundreds, for an average of 33, and in the latter part of the season he helped Lancashire II win the Minor Counties competition, scoring over 300 runs and averaging 50. He was a capped player, he was well liked, and at thirty-four he could look forward to another two or three seasons at least at Old Trafford. But when he got his contract for 1949, he found that the committee were offering him marginally less than most of the other capped players. He felt that all capped players should be treated alike, and with the sudden and perhaps unreasonable resentment that sometimes characterizes the outgoing, ebullient nature, he rejected it.

'Afterwards,' he says now, with engaging frankness, 'I thought, what a fool, just for the sake of a few quid. I could

have made that up with match money. I was thoroughly enjoying myself, and getting paid for it, and I should have had
another two or three years.' But any regrets are soon shrugged
off; he went back to enjoy another two or three seasons with
Norfolk, and he had never really seen himself as a professional
first-class cricketer anyway. Then his eyes twinkle. 'But I did
have one good week.'

During that winter, Lancashire signed Ken Grieves, the Australian all-rounder, and he went straight into the side when the
1949 season began. Meanwhile Geoffrey, off to an uncertain
start, was dropped. Thus when Lancashire went to Lord's at the
end of May, neither of the heroes of their victory twelve months
earlier was playing.

Relegated to the Seconds, Geoffrey was the only one to stand
up to a Yorkshire II attack that included Wardle and the leg-
spinner Leadbeater, and his innings of 80 regained him his
place. He promptly lost it again after a failure against Warwickshire, and he missed two more matches before being recalled against Kent, when one of the bowlers ranged
against him, Brian, was even less sure of his place than his
brother.

Although Brian had not made the progress hoped for in
1948, better times were ahead. But it was Geoffrey who re-
habilitated himself in this match. 'Edrich drove brother Brian
for four,' wrote Eric Todd in the *Manchester Evening Chronicle,*
'and took a single off Dovey to reach his 50. Never was a half-
century more warmly cheered, and gratefully accepted. The
prodigal had come home.' He made 90, and Todd added: 'I
give full marks to Edrich – "the man who came back".' These
comments show the affection in which Geoffrey was already held
in Lancashire.

From these unpromising beginnings, Geoffrey went on to
enjoy one of his best seasons, scoring more runs in the championship than any other Lancashire player and averaging 39.
He had developed into the ideal No. 3 – capable of scoring
quickly but safely, and a tenacious fighter when things went

95

wrong. 'Edrich,' said *Wisden* that year, 'generally played his best innings when most needed.'

The New Zealanders were here that year, and when Hutton, Washbrook, Bill Edrich and Compton were fit they were an automatic choice for England's first four. Bill played in all the Tests and averaged 54, and he averaged 40 for Middlesex; yet he had his days of failure, and he was not perhaps quite the force in county cricket that he had been in previous seasons. That Middlesex tied for the championship was due more to all-round strength than to the huge and rapid first-innings totals of 1947. His bowling certainly fell away, so much so as to become 'almost a negligible quantity', according to *Wisden*; but he was as alert as ever at slip and took 52 catches in the course of the season, second only to Laddie Outschoorn. Bill's brilliance at slip in his best years is apt to be forgotten.

In making 134 against Northamptonshire, he gained a new distinction by 'hitting' a nine. There were no restricted boundaries in those days, the wicket was pitched on the Tavern side, and with Vince Broderick bowling from the Nursery end, Bill played his famous lofted on-drive and it rolled up towards the Nursery clock with Dennis Brookes after it. Brookes was not the fleetest of movers, and Freddie Brown ran thirty yards towards him to intercept the throw. Then he flung the ball at the wicket at the pavilion end just as Syd Brown grounded his bat. They had already run five, and the ball was deflected to the pavilion rails for four more.

Brian played in 22 of Kent's 26 championship matches and enjoyed easily his best season so far. In fact he had one purple patch which few players can equal. He began with several scores in the forties, and he was also getting more bowling, which helped his morale. At Southampton on 4th June he took the first five Hampshire wickets to fall and finished with seven for 41, and although his chances with the ball were still limited by the success of Wright and Dovey, he went on picking up useful wickets. Two good knocks against Derbyshire of 37 and 46, the second when Copson, Gladwin, Jackson and Rhodes

Regaining the Ashes after twenty years: the scene at the Oval in August 1953 as Bill and Denis Compton leave the field

Above, left, an Edrich cut; right, an Edrich hook; *below,* Bill looks on apprehensively, fearing an unauthorised watering of the pitch, during the M.C.C. *v.* An Australian XI game at Melbourne, November, 1954

Brian goes round the
wicket for Kent

Below, Geoffrey makes the 327th of his 333 catches in first-class cricket,
May 1957. The batsman is Godfrey Evans

Immaculate forward defence from Brian; *below*, introduced to the President of the M.C.C. by acting captain Jack Davies at Canterbury, August 1949. On Brian's left are Godfrey Evans, Doug Wright, Arthur Fagg and Tony Pawson

were fighting to bowl their side back into the game, then put him in good order for the Tunbridge Wells week that followed.

On Saturday 25th June, in extreme heat, Sussex won the toss and batted until midday on the Monday after Kent had decided to rest the much overbowled Doug Wright. Declaring at 482 for nine, they proceeded to bowl Kent out for 237, of which Brian, batting No. 6, contributed 60, his highest score in first-class cricket. He doesn't remember doing anything consciously different, but he found he was playing his shots and really hitting the ball. Not surprisingly Kent were asked to follow on, and at stumps on that second day they were 22 for one.

The Nevill ground, enclosed by seats and marquees, had never looked lovelier than when Kent began their final-day task on the Tuesday morning in glorious weather. The bright green of the outfield, contrasting with the darker hue of the trees surrounding the ground, the bleached marquees, the pink of the rhododendrons, and the gay summer frocks, inspired one writer to call it 'the perfect English scene'. The days of the big crowds were not yet over, and the arena buzzed with excitement as Ames and Todd came out to resume Kent's innings at eleven o'clock. Unfortunately, the wicket – good enough at the start – was not lasting quite as well as the weather, and this no doubt contributed to what followed. In the first over Todd was bowled by the fast-medium left-arm Wood, and in the second Ames was brilliantly caught at the wicket off Jim Cornford. Three runs later, at eighteen minutes past eleven, Mayes was bowled for a duck, and that was 25 for four. Kent were still 220 behind, and everyone on the ground was bitterly regretting a wasted day.

As Brian joined Peter Hearn it was with the knowledge that all the stars had gone and they had nothing to lose. In the first innings the ball had come nicely on to the bat, and he had played his shots and got away with it. A couple of half-volleys from the medium-pacers put him in good heart now, and when Jim Langridge came on with his left-arm spinners he went down the track and drove him. The two left-handers had added

D 97

38 when Hearn failed to get quite to the pitch of Langridge and was caught at mid-on.

Langridge had found a dusty spot and the ball sometimes turned and lifted. Brian, advancing down the wicket, made up his mind to get it on the full whenever he could. But Clark, the Kent captain, after escaping a caught and bowled, was snapped up at second slip, and in came fast bowler Eddie Crush.

The Kent tail was a long one, and there was no real batting left. But Brian was now hitting the ball to all parts of the ground, and he reached his second fifty of the match before he lost Crush at 113 for seven. Kent were still 132 behind, with only Ray Dovey, Fred Ridgway, and reserve wicket-keeper Ward to come; but Dovey, too, attacked the bowling, and the terrors of the worn patch suddenly seemed to vanish. They put on 79, of which Dovey got 34, including a straight six off Langridge, before Dovey was caught on the edge by Ken Suttle.

That was 192 for eight, still 53 behind. But Ridgway settled in, Brian ran to his hundred in two hours ten minutes, and by lunch Kent at 221 for eight had wiped off all but 24 of their arrears.

Even now the potential extent of the recovery was hardly realised. But soon after lunch it was obvious enough. Against the Combined Services in an early-season pipe-opener, these two had given a glimpse of what they could do together by adding 74 for the last wicket. Now Ridgway hit a massive six on to the roof of the refreshment tent and between them they put on 51 in the first twenty minutes. Sussex, the pretensions of their attack fully exposed, would now have to bat again.

By three o'clock Brian and Ridgway were engaged in 'the biggest hitting seen on a Kent ground for years', as one paper put it. Altogether they put on 161 in 70 minutes, and when Ridgway was finally caught off James Langridge by brother John he had made 89, including four 6's and ten 4's. Brian was 173 not out, and Kent were 353 for nine, 108 ahead. And they weren't quite done with yet. Ward kept his end up while Brian went for the runs, and the score had reached 379 when

Ward was caught at silly mid-off, by which time Brian was 193 not out. Sussex needed 135 to win in 105 minutes, and the crowd were glad they came.

The excitement subsided as the Sussex openers put on 51, and Sussex had reached 99 for one when Brian came on and bowled John Langridge. He then had Charlie Oakes caught at mid-off, Dovey bowled Jack Oakes, and at 103 for four the game was alive again. Oh for Doug Wright! sighed the Kent supporters. And oh, too, for Godfrey Evans, as the unfortunate Ward fumbled chances which might have won the match. But it had been a memorable day's cricket, and no one minded overmuch when Sussex ran out winners by six wickets with ten minutes to spare.

Brian, said *Wisden*, had timed his left-handed strokes perfectly all round the wicket, 'and though the ball often turned quickly and rose nastily, he mastered the attack in great style.' Keeping the ball mostly on the ground, he hit twenty-nine 4's, and the nearest thing to a chance was a drive past mid-on to which Hugh Bartlett just got a hand. His match aggregate was 253 for once out, and he was awarded his county cap.

Bill, Geoffrey and Eric had all gained this distinction rapidly enough. But Brian, joining Kent in 1939, had waited ten years for it. 'Congratulations on county cap,' cabled Bill that night. 'Next step the England side.'

In the second match of the Tunbridge Wells week, against Gloucestershire, Kent again batted badly, and Brian could not rescue them this time. But when Gloucestershire had made 384 for five after dismissing Kent for 182, Brian changed his angle to round the wicket, reduced his pace, and took the last five wickets to fall for 15 runs, finishing with the excellent figures of 29 overs, 10 maidens, 7 for 68. Gloucestershire still won easily, but to take seven wickets in an innings twice in a month, for a bowler who didn't usually get on unless things stuck a bit, was a considerable feat.

In the return against Gloucestershire at Bristol, Brian put on 107 with Ames against Goddard and company when Kent were in desperate straits, but with Wright back in the side after his rest, and amateurs like Jack Davies and Tony Pawson available in August, an occasional score of 30 or 40 was not quite enough. 'The amateurs inevitably pushed me lower down the order,' he says, 'or even out of the side altogether. It's not easy to make runs at No. 7, knowing all the time that you're fighting for your place. I was also prone to muscle strains, presumably after the years of under-use, and I missed the odd game through that as well.

'We always had to reckon, in late July and August, that two or three of the younger players, the "strugglers", would have to make way for the amateurs. Personally I didn't resent this at all. Had we been getting enough runs we wouldn't have been dropped. And in any case they were good players. It was just unfortunate for us that they became available.' Nevertheless Brian, averaging 22 with the bat and taking 37 wickets, could look back with satisfaction on that 1949 season.

1950 was the year of Ramadhin and Valentine; but the first Test, at Old Trafford, was the significant one for Bill. The pitch proved responsive to spin from the start, and England were soon 88 for five, all to Valentine for 34. 'I'd had a look at Valentine in the MCC match at Lord's,' says Bill, 'and he spun the ball a lot and was very accurate, but I didn't think he was anything out of this world. I got 64 that day, but in the Test Match he got me for 7.' Bailey and Evans saved the day with a stand of 161, and England made 312. Then the West Indies fell to Berry and Hollies in their turn for 215, giving England a lead of 97; but Hutton was unfit to open, Simpson, Doggart and Dollery were soon out, and England were still only 140 ahead. It was at this point that Yardley joined Bill, and they stopped the rot by adding 65 before Yardley was out just before the close. Bill was then 51 not out.

205 ahead on a spinner's wicket, with six wickets still to fall, England had survived the crisis. With the wicket so much in favour of spin, a target of 250 was likely to be too much. Victory celebrations, of course, were premature, but something of this outlook was in Bill's mind that evening when he and

Godfrey Evans were invited to a party. The result was that he committed the indiscretion of arriving back in his hotel room some time after midnight.

Since he had earlier committed the indiscretion of allowing himself to be quartered in the room next to Bob Wyatt, chairman of selectors, his nocturnal high spirits, and the efforts of the night porter to remove his shoes, were duly noted and filed away for future reference.

Next morning Bill took his score to 71, drawing from *Wisden* the comment that he 'played gallantly for three hours ten minutes'. England went on to win comfortably; but Bill's innings didn't satisfy Wyatt. He took Bill out on to the committee-room balcony after the game and said : 'Have you anything to say about your conduct on Friday night ?'

'Anything to say ? What do you mean ?'

'I heard the night porter undressing you and putting you to bed.'

'Don't be bloody silly !' But the inference was clear enough. 'Was there anything wrong with my play ?'

'I didn't think you were batting as well on the Saturday morning as you did on the Friday evening.'

'Oh, come off it, Bob.'

'Well, I'm going to report you to Lord's.'

After his innings at Old Trafford, Bill could hardly be dropped. But at Lord's he fell cheaply twice to Ramadhin. 'At Old Trafford,' says Bill, 'where the pavilion is side-on and the light is good, I could see what Ramadhin was doing quite easily. But at Lord's, out of the pavilion background, I hadn't a clue.' In one of the most uncomfortable innings of his life, Bill batted 90 minutes in the first innings for 8, and did no better at the second attempt. The file on Old Trafford was dusted off and brought out, and Bill was dropped for the rest of the series.

Far worse, the vendetta against him was pursued. The first Bill knew of this was when he was asked to report to a self-appointed committee of three of the cricket hierarchy – Colonel R. S. Rait-Kerr, secretary of the MCC, 'Plum' Warner and

Harry Altham. 'We have a report here from the chairman of selectors,' they said, 'that you were drunk during a Test Match, and that your play was affected. What we'd like you to do is to withdraw your name from selection for Australia.'

'I'm certainly not going to withdraw. I want to go to Australia. I've done nothing seriously wrong. I've had a bit of an upset with Bob, but he's such a bloody Puritan.'

When the touring party was announced, Bill was not in it; yet he learned from Robins that the voting had been 11–2 in his favour. Who were the two against him? Robins would not name them, but Bill's guess was that one might be Brian Sellers and the other Freddie Brown. The latter as captain would have the final say. At the Scarborough Festival he confronted Sellers, who simply said: 'You'd better see Freddie.' So he invited Brown to his hotel room that night for a brandy. 'If it were left to me,' said Brown, 'I'd want you to go.'

So who was behind it? He still could not believe they'd go without him, and right up to the time when he saw them off on the train he still confidently awaited the telegram that never came.

Bill didn't play for England again for another three years. 'It amounted,' says Bill, 'to a three-year-suspension. I'd done an indiscreet thing, but it didn't warrant a punishment like that.'

Few cricketers put so much into their occupation as Bill did. His methods of relaxing and recharging his batteries were not untypical of his profession, although, with his strong constitution, and his love of a party (partly a left-over, perhaps, from the Mess parties of the war years), he carried them further than most. Not many years later it was acceptable for the captain of the winners of the County Championship to boast about the late-night sessions in which he and some of his team indulged. But in 1950, a small indiscretion like Bill's could ruin a career.

This was the second body-blow that the MCC was to deliver to one of its most loyal servants. Yet there were no complaints from Bill. He had transgressed, and he accepted his punishment, not knowing at the time how harsh it was to prove. His reply would be to go on making runs, so that they would have to recall him.

For that 1950–51 series in Australia, the England selectors cut off their noses to spite their faces. How sick the players themselves must have been at Bill's absence, from a series which he would almost certainly have turned England's way. And how sick those who left him at home must have been at the repeated criticisms of their error. This was not hindsight – Bill's omission was the one point of disagreement with the original selection, laboured *ad nauseam* by E. M. Wellings in particular. But he wasn't the only one. 'Edrich should be here,' said Crawford White. 'The Australians cannot understand why he was left behind.' And after the second Test L. N. Bailey wrote: 'We would have been two up in this series if it had not been for a selection blunder at Lord's last summer. One man, just one man, would have made all the difference . . . That man was Bill Edrich.' 'Edrich,' said R. C. Robertson-Glasgow, 'should have come on this tour.'

Curiously enough an injury to Bill, at about the time he was dropped, obscured the real reason for his omission. Bill, sensibly enough, said nothing, and few guessed at the truth. The omission passed into cricket history as one of the greatest selection blunders of all time; but the background suggests a lack of understanding of human character and temperament which is infinitely more culpable that any mere error of judgment.

In the County Championship, which Lancashire shared with Surrey, the most remarkable feature of that 1950 season was the emergence of Roy Tattersall as an off-spinner; he took 193 wickets and headed the first-class averages. And with his emergence came the grouping of a great triumvirate of close fielders whose work in the leg trap and at slip, said *Wisden*, 'had to be seen to be believed'. To Tattersall, Grieves fielded at leg slip, Ikin just behind square, and Geoffrey in front, and during the season they took 132 catches between them, Grieves 63, Geoffrey 38, and Ikin 31. And before the season was out, a second bowler emerged who was to owe at least as much to these three men over the years – Brian Statham. 'It was a joy being a Lancashire quick bowler in those days,' Statham has written. 'We had one of the best close-catching squads any county possessed in my time – Grieves, Geoffrey Edrich, Ikin, and Hilton. A batsman who gave a chance to that bunch and got away with it had the sort of luck that wins the football pools.'

Geoffrey was left out of the first match that year against Surrey, but he responded with three hundreds in the next four innings, and by the end of May demands for his inclusion in the Test Trial were being made in southern as well as northern circles. He did not quite maintain this form, finishing fifth in the county averages at 33.14; but his 70 against Yorkshire at Sheffield, after Lancashire had been sent in to bat, helped to win one of the greatest Roses matches ever, and another outstanding knock was his 89 off Sussex at Old Trafford, when the other batsmen coped so badly on a dry, turning wicket that the match was all over in a single day. 'There is a good deal of his distinguished brother in Edrich,' wrote Swanton that year. 'A similar physique, to begin with, a similar predilection for the drive, and among other mannerisms that trick of remaining poised after the stroke, with the bat following full through pointing the direction of the ball.'

Brian could not find a place in the Kent side at first, but when he did he was given a good run. And he played a useful part in a great win, Kent's first of the season, against Middlesex at Lord's in June. Twenty-eight behind on first innings, Kent finished the second day at 139 for five, still only 111 in front; but Brian, playing a staunch innings in the middle of the order, was still there. Next morning Bill tested him with a succession of bumpers, one of which Brian tried to hook only to top-edge it first bounce into the sight-screen. This gave Jim Sims an opening for one of those corner-of-the-mouth aphorisms for which he was famous. 'Good shot, Brian,' was all he said, but it convulsed everyone – or almost everyone. What Bill said is not recorded.

Middlesex eventually lost by 32 runs; but everything else in that match was overshadowed by Bill. Of his 111 in the first innings Swanton wrote: 'He was at the top of his form, hooking viciously, well over his strokes on the off side, and sometimes banging the ball back past the bowler.' And in the second innings, when Middlesex were chasing victory, he got 93 out of 138 before the tail folded up. During this innings he became the second man that season to reach 1,000 runs, Reg Simpson beating him by ten minutes. It was also the nearest he ever got to making a hundred in each innings.

Brian's day-to-day performances in 1950 had been disappointing in the extreme, but Kent persevered with him, and in 1951 he at last began to show some of the form of which they had always believed him capable. He played in all but one championship match, which helped his confidence enormously, and he scored 1,267 runs for an average of 26. Modest as this average might seem, only two Kent players exceeded it – Fagg and the young Colin Cowdrey. Brian saved Kent's faces in their match with the Minor Counties with his first hundred for the county, and a month later he got his second championship century, 104 against Glamorgan at Swansea, an innings that was to prove even more important to him than he realised at the time. He also got much more bowling, and he finished second in the championship averages, bowling 407 overs and taking 26 wickets at 26 runs each. A total of 25 catches set the seal on his establishment in the Kent side.

One game that year that Brian had cause to remember was the fixture with Middlesex at Canterbury in August. On a pitch affected by rain, and after a delayed start, Bill played the anchor role in stands with Robertson and Compton, and Compton, captaining Middlesex in a season in which he and Bill shared the leadership, declared at 208 for five, leaving Kent 55 minutes batting that night, in which they lost two wickets. Brian and Arthur Phebey were staying at a small Canterbury hotel, and after a few beers in the bar they were about to go to bed when there came a great knocking at the door. The intruders proved to be Bill with Jack Young. The bar had to be opened, and the party went on until four o'clock, when Brian and Arthur Phebey somehow managed to slink off to bed. What time the other two got their heads down they had no idea.

Neither of the two Kent men felt much like breakfast next morning, but they made their way to the ground at about half-past ten. There in the nets they found Bill, the sweat pouring out of him as he exhorted Alan Moss and Don Bennett to bowl faster and faster at him. That afternoon, according to *Wisden*, Bill 'gave another object-lesson in the art of playing spin bowling' (Bill 67, Wright 5 for 96), and Middlesex were able to build up a lead of 261 before Compton declared. Kent were then bowled out for 144.

In championship matches, although scoring only one century, Bill made 1,733 runs at an average of 45, and *Wisden*, commenting that he remained in a class above the ordinary, added: 'If the situation demanded caution or called for rapid progress Edrich filled both roles with great distinction.' Yet in five Tests against South Africa that year he could not once find a place.

Amongst the Edriches, though, 1951 belonged to Geoffrey. In all matches he scored seven hundreds, five in the championship, and one of the others was against the South Africans. 'I treasure that innings most of all,' he says. 'Because McCarthy "pinged" me when I was about 60 – he hit me flush on the head and I had to go off for a bit. I had about twenty minutes on the table, during which we lost three wickets to Hugh Tayfield, and I heard Stan Worthington, who was taking over from Harry Makepeace as coach, say: 'Are you ready to go back yet, Geoff?' I said I was, and I carried on and got a hundred. They'd made 403, but we got past their score.'

The satisfaction of those triple achievements was still in his voice. McCarthy that year was quick, and he bowled more than his share of bumpers, but Geoffrey finished up with 121. This was not one of those innings when things go well from the start. For long periods he was not timing the ball well. 'Yet,' wrote Denys Rowbotham, 'Edrich would not give in. He only watched

each ball more and more closely . . . He did not bring Lancashire the lead by mastery of his normally efficient technique. He
did so by unremitting determination, coolness, and unflagging
concentration. It reminded one of what a fine team man Edrich
is. No cause is lost for him. Would that more English players
had half his spirit.'

The sentiment was later echoed by Brian Statham. 'Geoffrey
. . . possessed the outstanding characteristic of all the Edrich
family – he had guts, guts and more guts. Nobody got his wicket
lightly.' The selectors made heavy calls on the Lancashire bowlers that year, but when it came to choosing a batsman the
vacancy went not to Washbrook or to Geoffrey but to Ikin.
The honour was well deserved; but it could just as easily have
gone to Geoffrey.

Lancashire finished third in the championship, and once
again close catching was the key to their success. The catching
figures were: Grieves 47, Geoffrey 34, Ikin 27. 'Roy Tattersall
was such a great bowler,' says Geoffrey, 'that you could keep
right up on the bat, because there weren't many players who'd
try to hit through you. For Gimblett and one or two others –
Bill, for instance – you'd give yourself a bit more room. But Roy
didn't put many off the line; he was a lovely bowler to field to.
If anybody did hit one through he'd always apologise, whether
it was his fault or not.'

The experiment of sharing the Middlesex captaincy between
Denis and Bill, begun in 1951, was continued in 1952, but it
'satisfied few people'. Matches were lost, said *Wisden*, which
with more tenacity might have been saved. Yet because of the
relationship between the two men, the arrangement worked
reasonably well. One of the best matches at Lord's that year
was again the one against Kent. Alan Shirreff started on the
Saturday by getting Brown and Bill for o and Thompson for
3, and Middlesex were all out for 171. But they responded
by dismissing Kent for 120, and then Bill, true to habit, got a
hundred in the second innings. Kent were set 357 to win in
five hours, and they chased the runs to the end before failing by

46. Their chief scorers were the left-handers Peter Hearn, 80, and Brian, 64.

Although Compton, troubled by his knee, was dropped from the England side that year (against India), and Bill was described as 'inconsistent', both averaged 36 for Middlesex, and Bill exceeded 2,000 runs in all matches. And by changing to off-spinners he made a welcome return to the attack, taking 41 wickets at 26 runs each.

For Kent, Brian was called upon to bowl hardly at all; but he did so well with the bat that his absence from several matches through a shoulder injury was a real handicap to the side. His best knock, for the second year running, was against Glamorgan, and again it was to prove significant. Joining Dickie Mayes on the first day when Kent were 151 for five, he helped to put on 221 in just over three hours, and both men topped the hundred. Playing in only 17 championship matches, he scored 816 runs and averaged 31 in his best season yet.

The outstanding Edrich that year, however, was again Geoffrey. 'In many respects,' said one account, 'Edrich was the batsman of the year for Lancashire. He often had to go in after one of the opening pair had failed, and he thrived on difficult situations.' *Wisden* agreed. '. . . he consistently found himself playing the part of opening batsman. Seldom did he fail.' If his chief merits remained consistency and application, he could suit his style to the game with much of the adaptability of Bill at his best, and he never shirked risking his wicket – as some batsmen did – in a victory chase.

Two of his best innings were played against Northamptonshire in August. Once he had applied to join them. Now he used all the strokes against them in an innings of 162, made out of 305 scored while he was at the wicket. No one else made runs, and for much of the time he was facing one of the bowlers he respected most – George Tribe. Thanks to Norman Oldfield, then playing for Northants, the visitors escaped defeat; but the tussle was resumed ten days later at Old Trafford. During the first two days nearly all the batsmen adopted safety-first tactics; but the Northants' declaration on the last day asked Lancashire to get

176 in 110 minutes. Using their seamers only, and keeping the over rate down, Northants worked their way steadily through the order, and when Berry joined Geoffrey at the start of the last over, seven were still needed. They got five of them in five balls, but Berry, facing the last ball, could only manage to scrape a single. The wicket-keeper dropped the fieldsman's return, however, and the winning run was scrambled before he could recover it. Geoffrey finished with 71 not out. 'Delightful batting by Edrich,' said *Wisden*, 'enabled Lancashire to accomplish the task.'

After leaving Old Trafford Eric had gone back to Norfolk, where he shared the duties of professional at Lakenham with C. S. R. Boswell, the former Essex player. But although he kept wicket brilliantly, he did not prove the consistent run-getter Norfolk had hoped. When he was in, however, he could still make batting look ridiculously easy, as he did on a Saturday in August 1949 against Kent II, when he got 170 not out. The only time he was not in complete command was in the course of a scene that must be unique on a county ground.

'A cow,' it was reported afterwards, 'entered the ground by way of the main gate and the pavilion.' It had escaped from the market. Ignoring the members on the pavilion terrace, two of whom beat such a hasty retreat that they overturned an iron bench into the lap of Jack Nichols, she cantered down the pavilion steps and on to the field as though entering a bullring.

'Keep her off the wicket!' shrilled Eric, not entirely out of self-interest. But this was easier said than done. 'For the next twelve to fifteen minutes,' said the report, 'all was confusion. Half a dozen drovers, one mounted on a bicycle, appeared in pursuit as the cow lumbered around and across the ground.' Spectators and players alike fled from each new danger zone, and soon the scorebox was jammed to capacity and the steps up to it were hidden by a jostling crowd, while scoreboard, sight screens and trees were converted into refuge points.

After further demonstrating her prowess by clearing a row of forms in National Hunt style before bringing down the roof of a small tent, the cow eventually escaped over or through a fence and disappeared into some adjoining allotments. 'Lakenham's cow,' concluded the reporter, 'certainly deserves her place in the annals of Norfolk cricket.'

So too, for different reasons, did Eric, and in 1950 he was much more consistent. But in 1951 he took a coaching appointment at Stowe School, and he played for the county very little after that. Hopes that Peter G. Edrich, a son of Uncle George, might carry on the tradition were disappointed; a tearaway fast bowler, he played in two county matches that year but bowled in only one of them, taking 0 for 55. And within a year or so Eric, still a bachelor when he went to Stowe, emigrated to New Zealand following an affair of the heart that went wrong; but not many years later he came back to marry the girl.

Early in 1953, Middlesex decided to end the sharing of the captaincy that few had found satisfactory and appoint Bill as sole captain, and Bill received many letters of congratulation. They were a trickle, however, compared to the shoal of telegrams and letters he was to receive later that year.

This was the year of Hassett's Australians, and despite the wonderful spirit that existed between the two teams, the Test Matches produced cricket as tense and exciting as any that had gone before. Lindwall, with 26 wickets in the series at 18 runs each, proved that he was still a great fast bowler, Hassett, Harvey and Morris all made runs in the Tests, and Miller did enough with bat and ball to remain a potential threat with both. But the England batting proved brittle, and vociferous demands for the return of Bill Edrich from all over the country were answered when he was chosen for the third Test at Old Trafford. He had been exactly three years in the wilderness, and the surge of genuine sentiment that greeted his recall must be one of the great consolations of his life.

Lindwall and Miller, of course, he knew of old, but the other Australian bowlers were completely strange to him when he opened the England innings with Hutton, and in that game he failed. The match, like the first two, was drawn, and Bill was retained. After a long sight of the Australian bowlers in the Middlesex match in mid-July (49 and 32), he faced a crisis on a rain-affected pitch at Leeds. After Australia had gained a first-innings lead of 99, Hutton and Graveney went cheaply. 'Then came Compton,' said *Wisden*, 'and he and Edrich faced very hostile bowling from Lindwall, Miller and Archer. They were subjected to a number of bumpers but remained together for two-and-a-quarter hours.' Bill's hooking of Lindwall that day, square and to mid-wicket, was thrilling to see, though some Australian commentators thought they detected a note of desperation in it. Keith Miller, however, knew better. 'It's a waste of time,' he said, 'bowling bumpers to Bill.'

Lindwall, though, wouldn't give in, and in the final Test at the Oval, when England were moving ponderously and almost imperceptibly towards the victory that would regain the Ashes for the first time for 20 years, he had one last fling. 'Edrich,' said *Wisden*, 'magnificently hooked two successive bumpers from Lindwall.' That was the moment when everyone knew that the Ashes were won. 'I have always maintained,' says Trevor Bailey, 'that seeing this little man hook Ray Lindwall was one of the most exhilarating sights I have ever witnessed on a cricket ground.'

In all matches that year Bill had 60 innings, scored 2,557 runs, more than anyone else, and averaged 47, finishing seventh in the averages. He was now thirty-seven, yet by general consent he was batting as well as ever.

Geoffrey was again the most consistent of the Lancashire batsmen, and he scored over 1,000 runs in the championship. 'To do so,' said the Lancashire Year Book, 'was a notable achievement,' since he missed the last six games through a broken bone in his wrist after making 109 consecutive appearances. The injury came one evening in August at Old Trafford, on a wicket that was soft on top and hard underneath; and the bowler was Frank Tyson.

Lancashire had batted first and made 163, and Northants had replied with 177. Then, with about forty minutes left on the evening of the second day, conditions were perfect for Tyson and he bowled flat out.

Lancashire-born, and rejected by his own county, Tyson had a score to settle, and this may have accounted for the exceptional pace that he generated that evening – 'the only time,' wrote Brian Statham, 'that I have seen him bowl at his Australian speed.' Lancashire were soon 13 for three. 'Geoffrey,' continued Statham, 'was batting overnight, when the wicket was at its nastiest, and he took a lot of punishment about the hands and body.' So terrifying did Tyson appear, in fact, that Dennis Brookes, captaining Northants, actually took him off before the forty minutes was up. 'Why did you do it?' he was asked afterwards. 'I thought he'd kill someone,' he said.

Tyson at Northampton on an easy-paced pitch, says Geoffrey, was just another bowler. 'This was one of the naughty ones. I could help the bouncer on its way, but I could never hook correctly, so I had to take it. But if the ball hits flesh you're all right. I never worried about that. The only areas that worried me were teeth, eye and temple.

'To me the hook is the greatest shot of all. There's not many good hookers about. I know several players who began their careers hooking the short ones but had to cut it out through too many top edges. That's the secret of batting – you play the shots you know you can play, and you cut out the others. That's why my cricketing idol as a boy was Herbert Sutcliffe; after he'd batted a bit he knew exactly which shot was safe and which wasn't. And he had the self-control to cut the dangerous shot out.

'Cutting was my favourite shot, but if the ball is coming through unevenly, or keeping low, it's a dangerous shot. It's got to be coming through at a uniform height. Playing the shot is still a temptation, but you've got to resist it. I think if you're a dedicated player you can do that. It's easy enough to get out – anybody can do that.'

The morning after Tyson's great burst of speed, Geoffrey batted with a bruised hand that he didn't know was broken and made 81 not out, out of a total of 141. 'Great knock,' said

Washbrook when Geoffrey returned to the pavilion. Only two other batsmen, both tail-enders, reached double figures. But Northants finally won in a tremendous finish by one wicket.

Top score of 77 against Bedser, Surridge, Laker and Lock in John Ikin's benefit match was another good knock, but he reserved his best performance of all that year for the Roses match at Sheffield, where his first innings 65 was again top score. He had never made a hundred against Yorkshire, but in the second innings he got into the nineties against Trueman, Wardle and Illingworth before Nigel Howard, skippering Lancashire, told him he had one more over to do it. Wardle was bowling, and Geoffrey blasted one only to be caught at cover. His 92 was made out of 159 for seven.

Thus in that 1953 season Geoffrey was by no means overshadowed by Bill's return to the international scene; and indeed when George Duckworth took a Commonwealth side to tour India and play five unofficial Tests, Geoffrey was one of the party, alongside such players as Reg Simpson, Roy Marshall, Alan Watkins, Frank Worrell, Jack Iverson, Sam Loxton, Peter Loader and Sonny Ramadhin. He played 21 innings and averaged 40, but he did little of note in his three Tests.

For one Edrich – Brian – 1953 was not so happy. The shoulder injury that had marred what should have been his best season the previous year had not mended, he found he had lost his rhythm, and worse still he couldn't put anything into his bowling and had lost his nip off the pitch. He had never been a really long thrower, but he had always been able to get the ball in from the ring; now he couldn't let it go at all. After a bad start he was promoted to No. 3 to change his luck and at once got a 50, but he couldn't keep it up. By mid-July he had been dropped, his batting failures put him right back where he had begun, and without his bowling it was nothing like good enough.

'I had played pretty well in 1952,' he says, 'I'd tightened my defence up, and I'd ironed out some of my weaknesses, although I still got out through hitting across the line. I liked the sweep too much, and although I got a lot of runs from it, it also got me out. But the runs had to come from somewhere, and the question arises, when does a shot stop being economic? I used to stick my right leg up the track and hit across, and sometimes I missed, and in those days the front foot didn't make the difference it did later. I got out through hitting the ball in the air, and I got out through trying to hook. They began to *think* me out, too. But I got myself out more than I was got out. With what I know now about coaching, I think most of my faults could have been eliminated.'

Miserable season for him though it was, the thought that he might not be retained for the following year did not occur to him. So when the news reached him, not in a personal interview but through a newspaper report, the shock was traumatic. He and Dickie Mayes, who had joined Kent the same day fourteen years earlier, had been sacked together. A letter signed by all his team-mates to say that they thought he'd always been a great team man and that his sacking was unfair eased the hurt, but it could not ease his worries. Married seven years earlier, he had two young children. He was only thirty-one, and he had hoped for another few years in the first-class game; although he wanted to stay in cricket in some capacity he had no plans of any kind. He was still in a state of shock a few days later when he had a phone call from Bill.

'How do you get on with Wilf Wooller?' asked Bill. Since not everybody hit it off with him, the question had to be asked.

'All right.'

Bill had met Wooller at a cricket dinner, and Wooller had asked him what Brian was doing now he was finished with Kent. 'I'm not sure,' said Bill, 'I haven't seen him.' 'Well,' said Wooller, 'he always gets runs against us. We're interested in him.'

No player is more respected than the one who always seems to get runs against your team. Brian was offered quite good terms, better than he'd been getting with Kent. It pulled him right up off the floor.

He told Wilf Wooller straight away about his shoulder, and

that his bowling seemed to be permanently affected. But Wooller wanted him as a batsman.

'The cricket season of 1954,' said the *Lancashire Year Book*, 'bad almost throughout the country, will not be forgotten for a very long time in Lancashire.' A total of $57\frac{1}{2}$ hours' cricket was lost by the county, and while batsmen struggled on soft, slow wickets, fieldsmen shivered in the cold. Bill, with six hundreds and an average of 39, did better than most, but after a single failure he lost his place in the England side against Pakistan. Yet his skill and tenacity seemed undiminished. 'I've seen the greatest,' said umpire Frank Lee to Geoffrey when they met early that August.

'What's that?'

'I saw your brother carted off the field, and I thought, we won't see Bill any more in this match.' Bill had tried to hook Tyson and had got a top edge on to the cheek-bone. He spent the night in hospital. Next morning the umpires were at the ground at ten-thirty as usual, and the first chap they saw coming from the pavilion, smoking a pipe, was Bill. 'What's the wicket like, Frank?' he asked. As soon as a wicket fell he was in, and his first ball from Tyson struck him over the heart. 'Edrich,' said *Wisden*, 'resumed batting on the last day and showed customary steadfastness.' His selection soon afterwards for the 1954–55 tour of Australia was widely applauded.

Geoffrey, with 1,202 runs at an average of 30, was one of only three Lancashire batsmen to score 1,000 runs that year, or indeed get anywhere near it. He did not get a hundred until mid-July, but he chose Pakistan for the honour, his 134 bringing Lancashire close to victory in a match they eventually lost.

It was Peter Walker who first said that all county players believe their actual figures underestimate their true value to their side. But whether Geoffrey believed this or not, it was certainly true of him. Loyal and unselfish in all he did, he lost a chance of two hundreds in a match against Nottinghamshire at Trent Bridge (167 not out and 84) through pressing for the victory that was just out of reach, and many of his best knocks were played in low-scoring matches on bad wickets, when 40 or 50 were worth so very much more. He remained an indispensable member of the close-catching unit supporting Tattersall, Statham, Berry and Hilton, and he threw himself heart and soul into the extended coaching scheme which was becoming such an important part of the Old Trafford scene, passing the highest MCC coaching examination. His benefit, to be taken in 1955, was, in the words of the *Year Book*, 'earnestly recommended to all'. He had, they said, been a 'bulwark', whose orthodox determination and fighting qualities had been particularly valuable in that season of bad wickets.

After a bright start, Brian found the soft wickets difficult to adjust to, especially in Wales, where the ball never seemed to him to come on to the bat. But so far as Wooller was concerned he was a pleasing personality, popular with the other players, and judgment on him, in such an unkind season, was suspended.

Thus the three Edriches, Bill, Geoffrey and Brian, were now scattered to the north, south and west. The symmetry of an Edrich at all points of the compass was achieved during that season, however, when a new star appeared in the east.

Coached, like Eric and Bill before him, by F. E. Scott, who had now become Headmaster at Bracondale, John was playing for the Norfolk Junior Colts at thirteen, in 1950, and two years later he captained them. In 1953 he played in a full Norfolk Trial, along with another newcomer named Peter Parfitt, and they both showed up well. During the season John started to get centuries for the Club and Ground; but most of his cricket outside school that year was played for the Church of England Young Men's Society (CEYMS), a Norwich side skippered by Laurie Barratt, then the Norfolk captain. Now, in 1954, he was selected to play in Norfolk's first two championship matches.

At seventeen John, although extremely boyish-looking, was well developed physically; yet he hardly seemed mature enough for county cricket, any more than Bill had done at sixteen in that match against All-India twenty-two years earlier. The impression was hardly removed by his batting failures in the first two matches; but Norfolk persevered with him, and in his first county match at Lakenham he was sent in on a rain-affected pitch at 50 for three.

The not-out batsman was Bill Drinkwater, also a CEYMS player, which helped to give John confidence. 'At the other end,' said a report, 'Edrich was clearly and understandably bent on getting himself acclimatised before attempting anything adventurous.' The Norfolk committee had judged his progress aright; and how many more of John's innings since then have started on exactly this note.

Rain spoiled his chances on that occasion, but in the next match, against Buckinghamshire, he got 56, at a time when the side was facing a rout. 'The main honours,' said the *Eastern Daily Press,* 'went to Edrich. He played some delightful strokes on the off and straight in a stay of 145 minutes.' The writer noted, however, that he consistently failed to connect with the ball that went through outside the leg stump; and a contemporary recalls that he had a similar weakness outside the off stump, where club bowlers generally chose to attack him. These were faults that were to take him years of thought and practice to eliminate.

Clearly though, the basic ability was there, and although 56 remained his best score that year he topped the averages and established himself as the best batting prospect produced by Norfolk since the war. National Service was looming up ahead, but he could expect another full season before his call-up, and he was a young man who knew exactly what he wanted: he had his eye on the first-class game. Geoffrey put in a word for him at Old Trafford, but by that time they were recruiting Lancastrians only, and in any case with Ikin, Wharton, Pullar and Barber they felt they had enough left-handers already. The next possibility seemed to be Middlesex, and Bill certainly wanted him there; but both John's father, Fred Edrich, and Bill senior, encouraged him to go where he would not risk the taint of favouritism, or of being overshadowed by his cousin. He decided on Surrey, Norfolk recommended him, and Surrey gave him a contract which guaranteed him at least another two seasons at the Oval after he had completed his National Service.

Bill knew it would be his last tour of Australia, and some relaxation may have crept in. He hardly played an innings of any substance against the State sides, and he did not score heavily in the Tests; yet Hutton's faith in his fighting qualities was such that he retained him in the side until the Ashes were won. Thus Bill played in the first four Tests, and in a low-scoring series dominated by Tyson and Statham he did not let Hutton down. When England were fighting to save the Brisbane Test he put on 124 with Peter May, and his 88 was easily the highest individual score of the innings. For the third and fourth Tests he opened with Hutton and took part in the only first-wicket partnerships of any note for England in the series, and it was not until the tension was off that he was replaced by Tom Graveney. By the end of the tour, though, it was clear that his Test Match career, so wantonly interrupted at its peak, was over.

Just as the era of Hendren and Hearne had been about to pass twenty years earlier, so now the dominance of Compton and Edrich seemed about to end. Compton, it is true, was still an England player, but in the county game the so-called Middlesex twins were no longer the feared destroying agents they had been for so long. For Middlesex in 1955, Compton averaged 31 and Bill 26, and Bill always seemed to be struggling to find his form. Brian, too, was finding it no easier to get runs for Glamorgan than he had done for Kent. But neither Middlesex nor Glamorgan had young players ready to replace them.

One county that had been busy rebuilding from within was Lancashire, and one of the men who was working hardest to bring on the young men who must one day replace him was Geoffrey. He began his benefit year badly by cracking two bones in his right hand in a trial match; but by the time the county season had got properly under way he was fit enough to be recalled. By the beginning of June, with 31 and 103 against Kent, his place was no longer in doubt.

For his benefit match he had chosen Derbyshire, the match which Pollard had chosen six years earlier, and Pollard had received £8,000; but Geoffrey's reward, in the words of the Year Book, was 'a saddening experience for one who has done so much for the county'. The game was played in indifferent weather, but it didn't actually rain, so there could be no insurance claim. By this stage of the 1950s the post-war interest that had filled the cricket grounds was falling off, and on the Saturday large numbers stayed at home to watch the televised Wimbledon finals. Geoffrey did have the satisfaction of adding 157 with Grieves after Lancashire had reached 46 for three, and Lancashire won; but nothing could compensate for the experience of being the least fortunate of all the Lancashire players who had taken benefits since the war. An averagely good benefit at that time for a Lancashire player of equivalent service was £6,000; Geoffrey got £3,575.

A month later Geoffrey was dropped, under circumstances which hurt him deeply. Following on 173 behind in the Roses match at Sheffield, Lancashire cleared the arrears thanks to Washbrook, but it needed stern defence from Geoffrey (37 not out in two hours), to save the game. 'Well played, Geoff,' said the other players when he returned to the pavilion. But Washbrook said: 'You're playing for the Two's tomorrow at Keswick.' Perhaps the news had upset him too; and in any case the decision had no doubt been made before Geoffrey's innings. But Geoffrey had never really hit it off with Washbrook, and the timing rankled. 'All right,' said Geoffrey to himself, 'I'll show them.' Nothing less than a hundred would be good enough, he knew, and in this, his only knock for the Seconds that year, he got 111, forcing his way back into the side.

At the end of that 1955 season, Winston Place, four years older than Geoffrey, was not re-engaged, and with young players like Jack Dyson, Roy Collins, Geoff Pullar, Jackie Bond, and the amateur Bob Barber coming along, the pressure on the older players was bound to increase. But Geoffrey, highly regarded by the Lancashire committee, had met the challenge, and for the moment his future seemed secure.

The brightest future of all at that time, of course, seemed to lie with John; in 23 innings for Surrey II in the Minor Counties competition he scored 762 runs for an average of 45. But Surrey were immensely strong, and to his disappointment he could not find a place in the county side. In Norfolk he had been a big fish in a little pond. Now his successful days at the wicket went unnoticed. The complete opposite of Eric, Bill and Brian, and even of Geoffrey, he was of dour, reserved temperament, and he made friends far less readily. 'On many a lonely night,' he says in his book, 'I asked myself if I had done the right thing in moving to London. I felt homesick, and in the almost anonymous setting of the junior side, despite the genuine friendliness, I sometimes felt lost.'

Ask any Middlesex player what his side's prospects were in this period and he would say: 'It depends on Denis and Bill.' And so far as the batting was concerned it still did. Had Compton been able to play a full season in 1956, Middlesex might have done even better than the fifth place they achieved. But Compton played in only eight championship matches, and it was a rejuvenated Bill, fresh from a winter's rest, who led the batting and topped the averages. In a wet season in which only two batsmen reached 2,000 runs he made 1,831 and averaged 33, and *Wisden*, critical of his performance in 1955, changed their tune entirely. 'Edrich, at the age of forty, showed no decline in ability.' And in a year when the face of the Middlesex side changed considerably, they complimented him on his captaincy and thought he brought the best out of the young players.

At least four of Bill's innings that year are worthy of recall. After doing little more than get his eye in for the first few matches, he played a superb innings of 208 not out at Chesterfield, made in five hours off Jackson, Gladwin and company and including four 6's and thirty-two 4's. No one would have guessed that in the previous year he had seemed on the verge of retirement. Then, galvanised perhaps by the return of Denis Compton in mid-summer, he helped to make Maurice Tremlett's benefit at Glastonbury memorable in a thrilling stand with his old partner. 'Everything else in the match was overshadowed by the batting of Compton and Edrich,' said *Wisden*. 'It was reminiscent of their great days of 1947 . . .' This was only Compton's second match after his knee operation, and he made 110 in three hours; but it was Bill who started it with a grand 89.

Of an entirely different but not untypical kind was Bill's knock against the Australians a fortnight later. Here the opposing captain was his old adversary Ray Lindwall, and neither man gave much away. After the Australians had made 207 on a soaked pitch, and Middlesex had lost three for 14, Bill held one end while Compton made a brilliant 61 out of 77, then went on to provide the stuffing of the innings by batting five hours twenty minutes for 84. Richie Benaud, on his first tour of England, finished off the innings, but the game was drawn.

Perhaps Bill's best performance that year was at the Oval against Surrey, where Laker and Lock in that period were almost invincible. Shot out for 69 on a green pitch by Loader, Middlesex found themselves 107 behind when they batted again. This time the ball was turning, and of the first eight Middlesex batsmen, none reached double figures except Bill. *Wisden* spoke of 'an innings of technical skill and immense concentration by Edrich', in which he 'demonstrated how the turning ball should be played'. In four-and-a-quarter hours he made far and away the top score of the match with 82.

So much dour application deserved an innings of relaxation, and this came at the Scarborough Festival for the Gentlemen against the Players. He opened the innings against Tyson and Moss and set the mood of the whole game with an exhilarating display of controlled hitting, his 133 including four 6's and sixteen 4's; and even in the second innings, when he top-scored with 43, he stood out from the other 'amateur' players.

Another Edrich was meanwhile earning praise as a captain: Geoffrey. Indeed, one of the most remarkable features of that 1956 season was his captaincy of Lancashire in the frequent absences of Cyril Washbrook, first on selection duties and then on his recall to the England side. John Ikin, the senior professional, would have been the automatic choice, but he was injured. 'My first game as captain was against Glamorgan at Old Trafford,' recalls Geoffrey. 'I'd never skippered a side of any kind before in my life, and I had one or two butterflies in my stomach. But things went right, the side responded well, and we rolled Glamorgan up by tea-time on the second day. The only chap who really stuck us up in both innings was Brian. He didn't make many runs, but he was always a hard man to get out.'

The battle for the County Championship that year was a thrilling one, with Surrey and Lancashire the chief contenders; and there is no doubt that the Lancashire side enjoyed playing under Geoffrey and responded eagerly to his lead. Against Derbyshire he declared 87 ahead but could not engineer the collapse that was wanted. He set Essex 203 to win in 150 minutes but they declined the challenge, and then, in the return, with Statham away, he put them in on a green top and finished three behind on first innings but won the match. In the next match Lancashire became the first team ever to win a first-class match without losing a wicket. After Leicestershire had been dismissed for 108, Lancashire declared at 166 without loss, shot Leicestershire out for 122, and knocked off the runs again without loss.

Sent in to bat by Nottinghamshire at Liverpool, Geoffrey declared at 207 for seven after a blank second day, dismissed Notts for 86, declared his second innings after one ball, and left Notts 122 to get in 98 minutes. 'Geoffrey, I'll bowl right through at one end,' said Brian Statham; and Notts, with twenty-one minutes to go, were 81 for seven. At this point Geoffrey risked a few overs of Greenhough's leg-breaks, but Notts refused the bait and held out.

This aggressive captaincy had such rewards that twice Lancashire gained a clear lead in the championship. Everything seemed to depend on the match at the Oval against Surrey. But although they dismissed Surrey for 96 and reached 40 for two, rain intervened, and Surrey, luckier with the weather than their rivals, ran to their fifth successive championship under Surridge.

For Cyril Washbrook, with his many other preoccupations that season, the experience of returning to a side which had reacted with such enthusiasm to his deputy must have been slightly deflating. 'When the skipper was away,' wrote John Kay, 'Lancashire lost nothing in leadership because of the thorough way Edrich assumed responsibility. Always a fighter, the Norfolk man had the rare gift of remaining one of the boys yet stepping up to boss the show without loss of prestige or dignity. The younger players leaned heavily on Edrich and whilst it would be unkind to say that Washbrook was not missed, there were compensating features about the side's cricket when Edrich was in command.' Of the ten matches in which Geoffrey acted as captain, six were won, first innings lead was gained in three of the other four, and the only match where no points were gained was in the return with Glamorgan, where play was limited to three-and-a-half hours. Thus in 10 out of 28 matches, 84 out of the county's total of 180 points had been gained. Ken Grieves and Alan Wharton, writing in the Manchester evening papers, paid generous tributes to Geoffrey. 'He has it in him,' said the Australian Grieves, 'to become a great captain.' And he added: 'The side he leads will be a happy one.'

Following the wash-out at the Oval, the side moved down to Hove for the last match of the season, against Sussex. Lancashire could not now win the championship, but by gaining first innings lead they could make certain of being runners-up. It was in this atmosphere that an attempt to drop Geoffrey to make room for another player met with open rebellion. 'If you leave Geoff out,' said John Ikin, 'I'm not playing, so you'll be left with ten men.' Whatever Washbrook's instructions may have been, he relented; but the story got back to Geoffrey, and he set his teeth. When an Edrich does that, something or someone is bound to suffer. Sure enough he batted for four hours, made a century, and saved Lancashire from complete collapse on a wicket that was taking spin after overnight rain. Thanks to him Lancashire got 295, dismissed Sussex for 238 to get the points they wanted, and were well on the way to victory when rain spoilt the last day.

On the second night of this match, a Lancashire supporter from Rochdale named Bill Collins gave a cocktail party in his hotel to celebrate the achievement of coming second, and Washbrook was called upon to make a short impromptu speech in reply, in which he paid tribute to the leading players. Afterwards Malcolm Hilton asked if he could have a word. 'Our skipper's had a chat,' he said, 'but he's missed one person out, and we'd like to thank Geoff Edrich.' Asked next day by Washbrook what he meant by intervening, Hilton replied simply : 'Well, you didn't mention Geoff.'

It was obviously difficult for Washbrook to appreciate what Lancashire owed when he was absent to his deputy; but an echo of the impact Geoffrey made on the side was provided many years later by another great Lancashire captain, Jackie Bond. Speaking of his four great cricketing heroes, all like himself on the small side – Lindsay Hassett, Eddie Paynter, 'Buddy' Oldfield, and Geoffrey – he told Eric Todd that Geoffrey's ability as a player and influence on his men whenever he was acting captain had made a profound impression on him and set him a standard of leadership and efficiency at which to aim when he was appointed captain in 1968.

In a season of low scores Geoffrey had only a moderate record with the bat, but he got his 1,000 runs, average 26, and he finished fifth in the championship averages. To add to this he led the Lancashire catchers with 33 against Grieves' 31 and Hilton's 28.

For Bill and Geoffrey, then, it was a season to be savoured. It seemed that Bill had plenty of first-class cricket left in him, while some saw in Geoffrey the future captain of Lancashire. But Brian, cheerful as ever in adversity, had been having his usual struggle to survive. Wooller had given him every chance, finally trying him as an opener, but long before the end of that season it was plain that his first-class career was in jeopardy. The gap of the war years had proved too wide a crevasse to jump.

It was then that Wooller broached the subject of coaching. 'We've got a bit of money in the kitty,' he said, 'and we want to promote cricket in Wales. We want somebody to take over coaching at various centres throughout Wales while still on the playing staff. Would you be interested?'

Would he! All through his career he had done various stints of coaching, and he now had his MCC coaching certificate. No doubt if he carried on in county cricket he would still have his ups as well as his downs, but with this appointment he could really look forward to the future. And he would still get plenty of cricket, playing for and in time skippering Glamorgan II.

Bill began the 1957 season consistently enough, with several useful scores, but his form fell away as the season progressed and he averaged only 23. 'As the years went by Bill lost some of his freedom,' says Trevor Bailey, 'and though, because of his sound technique, he was never easy to dismiss, it was possible to keep him relatively quiet by bowling a full length on and just outside the off stump – something which could never have occurred in 1947.'

The vacuum so confidently forecast in the Middlesex batting line-up arrived with a vengeance when, at the end of that season, Compton announced his retirement because of his knee. Bill, still remarkably fit at forty-one, believed his form would return, and he had no thought yet of retiring; but he decided to give up the captaincy. After sharing the honour with Compton for two seasons, he had captained Middlesex for five years on his own.

What was he like as a captain? Whenever there had seemed the smallest chance of victory, he had always striven for it, and this is reflected in the results he achieved, which show an extraordinarily low proportion of draws compared with other counties. His methods often lifted Middlesex to a higher place in the championship table than their relative merit strictly deserved.

Wisden, it will be remembered, had applauded the way he brought on the young players. And one of the most experienced of all county captains, Wilf Wooller, later wrote this of him, as batsman, captain, and man :

> I played many times against Bill Edrich at his best. He was a tremendous fighter and was never disturbed by any form of pressure put on him by an opposing captain. In fact any nonsense made him more determined than ever to stay at the crease.
>
> One shot in particular was disconcerting and might well be used most profitably today – the lofted on-drive. Any in-ducker pitched around middle and leg he picked up and hit over mid-on for 4, or occasionally 6.
>
> I also regarded him as a pretty shrewd thinker on the game. There are those who understand the tactics of the contest and those who play by ear. Bill was in the first category, and his brilliant partner of so many stands Denis Compton was in the second. For that reason he made a captain who always had to be respected on the battlefield.

Bill played one more season, but he did little of note in thirteen championship matches, and his only hundred was for MCC against Cambridge University. When the offer came to captain Norfolk in the Minor Counties competition in 1959, it opened up an entirely fresh vista for him, and with Middlesex signifying their readiness to let him go, he was thrilled to accept.

He had actually played his maiden first-class innings 24 years earlier, in 1934; and in 964 innings he had made 36,965 runs, putting him high in the list of run-getters, with 86 hundreds and a career average of 42.19. He had also taken 479 wickets at an average of 33.31, not to mention 522 catches.

But Bill was a popular cricketer not so much for his successes as for his repeated triumphs over prejudice and adversity. His pugnacity and aggression, allied to the serene temperament and natural manners which characterised all the Edriches, were there for all to see. When his name hit the headlines because of his occasional domestic difficulties, brought about as much by his absences on overseas tours as by his way of life, the public sympathised rather than condemned.

He was known to be a man who lived hard and played hard. The public liked that too. 'Bill loved parties,' says Trevor Bailey, 'and he brought to them the same zest and enthusiasm which epitomised his cricket. He was also firmly of the opinion that a good one should never end before dawn.' His repertoire of songs, rendered in a husky baritone that only just carried, had been acquired during long-forgotten wartime nights in the Mess. He also did a conjuring trick as a party piece involving an egg, which, according to Bailey, 'was always far more entertaining when it failed than when successful, a view not shared by one distinguished cricket correspondent whose white tuxedo never looked quite so immaculate again.'

Geoffrey Howard, manager on Bill's last tour, recalls a party soon after they arrived in Australia at which Bill, rather too late in the evening, insisted on making a speech. What its content was no one ever knew – they could see his lips moving, but no sound whatever was coming out. 'I can still see the young Colin Cowdrey,' says Howard, 'on his first tour of Australia, standing open-mouthed in sheer astonishment.'

Geoffrey Edrich had begun the 1957 season as one of the most experienced men in the Lancashire side; he had scored nearly 15,000 runs for Lancashire and made 26 centuries, more than any other contemporary Lancashire player except Washbrook. But in a couple of months he would be thirty-nine. A fully qualified MCC coach, liked and admired by everyone at Old Trafford, he was an obvious candidate for appointment, before his playing days were over, to the captaincy of the Second XI. The only question was, at what point should such an appointment be made.

Early in the 1957 season the Lancashire committee decided that the time was now. Geoffrey continued to appear for the senior side when required, and he played some useful innings, but his main objective became to bring on the younger players. The results exceeded all expectations, the Second XI attaining seventh place out of thirty-two in the Minor Counties competition in what was very much an experimental year. Geoffrey, of course, had some excellent material to work on, including young men like Peter Marner and Brian Booth as well as those already mentioned. He himself proved the outstanding batsman, and his qualities of leadership again provoked the comment that he ought to be skippering Lancashire. Had he succeeded Washbrook at this time, wrote John Kay later, 'Lancashire cricket could have bloomed gloriously, because he had tended the garden so well. The youngsters worshipped him, they admired his fighting qualities and his desire to share their joys on and off the field.'

But that was a dream not even Geoffrey himself entertained. However, at the end of the 1957 season the Lancashire committee showed their appreciation. 'Edrich,' said the *Year Book*, 'set the side a splendid example, and took a very real interest in the development of the young professionals; the full fruits of the Committee's policy will it is hoped be seen over the next three seasons.' During this period, they announced, Geoffrey was to continue to lead the side, and he would also act as assistant coach to Stan Worthington. The inference was that he was being groomed to succeed him.

The end of that 1957 season saw the retirement of John Ikin, who returned to play and coach for Staffordshire; and Washbrook's retirement followed at the end of 1958. That Geoffrey as a potential first-eleven captain may still have been in the committee's mind was suggested when he was chosen to captain Lancashire against Northamptonshire when Washbrook was away and Barber was not available; but the game hardly got started through rain, and the opportunity was not repeated. He went back to skippering the Seconds, raising them to fourth place in the competition.

For 1959 Lancashire appointed Barber as captain, and they put the clock back by booking him in to a different hotel when the team were playing away, exactly the opposite of the example of friendly sociability set by Geoffrey. The two policies must have been uneasy bedfellows, and this may have accounted to some extent for the tragedy that followed.

Successful leadership can be contained in so many types of

The seventeen-year old John Edrich batting in a Surrey trial at the Oval, April 1955; *below*, John's first appearance in an All-Edrich XI in the same year: back row, l to r: Arthur E., Peter G., George C., Alan W., John H.; front, George H., W.J., W.A., G.A., Barry G., B.R.

'We haven't seen you before, have we?
The introduction was soon made.
Trueman *v.* Edrich, 1959

'It was my own fault . . .'
Hit on the side of the head
by Peter Pollock in the
First Test *v.* South Africa
at Lord's, July 1965

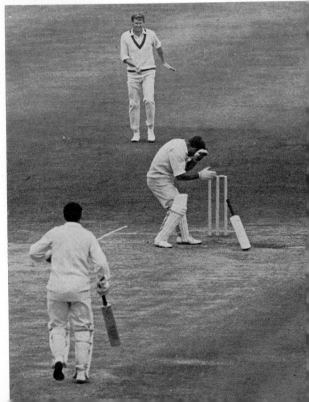

England 366 for 1 at the end of the first day's play *v.* New Zealand at Leeds, July 1965 (Edrich 194 not out, Barrington 152 not out). The Pollock incident, opposite, came nineteen days later

John and Brian opening for the
Edrich XI against the Lord's
Taverners at Ingham, September
1963; *below,* a typical John
Edrich square drive

personality that it is no criticism of Washbrook, or of Barber, to say that Geoffrey's methods were different. Certainly to be one of the boys and yet to retain control, as John Kay had pointed out, is given to few men. But Geoffrey happened to be one of them.

He himself was of quiet, unobtrusive temperament, and he never thrust himself forward. The traumas of the war years, perhaps, had left him lacking in self-confidence on formal occasions; but otherwise he was the easiest and most relaxing of companions, as those who toured with him have averred.

Geoffrey enjoyed his pint of beer, like his brothers, but he did not drink a lot. Two or three jars at the end of a day's play, and the usual thrash on a Saturday night when the team were playing away from home, was his habit. But early in the 1959 summer he went to a party given by Malcolm Hilton, who had always been one of his closest friends in the side. (It was Hilton who had spoken up that day at Hove.) Olga had just started a hairdressing business in Norfolk, and when Geoffrey drove home after the party it was to his digs. He had got home and was just going into the digs when a young policeman rode up on a bicycle.

Geoffrey was the last fellow to give trouble. This was before the breathalyser, and he accepted the police doctor, instead of demanding his own. After he was charged he reported the incident at once to the Lancashire committee, and he was told to plead guilty and there would be no publicity. He lost his licence for a period, but everyone at Old Trafford was extremely understanding and he believed the incident would be forgotten.

Three weeks later he took the Second Team to play Warwickshire II at Edgbaston, and they stayed in a guest house. Three members of the side – two senior players and one junior – came in late and had some difficulty in flushing the toilet. Geoffrey was called out of bed by Malcolm Hilton, and he hoisted Hilton up to try to clear the trouble, as the cistern was overflowing. They mopped up the mess afterwards, and Geoffrey thought no more about it. But unknown to him, some of the water had seeped through and damaged the decorations on the lower floor.

One member of the party – not a player – was told about the damage; but instead of reporting it to Geoffrey he apparently told the landlady that if she had any complaints to make them to Old Trafford. She took his advice.

When he got back to Old Trafford Geoffrey was summoned before the committee. 'We don't want your services any more,' he was told at the end of the interview. The explanation was that he was not a fit person to be in charge of young players.

The two incidents, coming one on top of the other, may have had a cumulative effect; but in retrospect it is difficult to see how a mature committee could possibly have perpetrated such an injustice. For Geoffrey it was a blow of shattering proportions, the destruction of his entire career, and for a long time he was suicidal. Adopted by the northern county as one of their own, and hitherto the committee's blue-eyed boy, he suddenly knew what it was to have the door slammed in his face.

After thirteen years of loyal service, he was offered no gentleman's agreement to leave at the end of the summer. He must pack his bags now, and leave in disgrace.

Geoffrey Howard, the Lancashire secretary, was a fervent admirer of all the Edriches; but there was nothing he could do about it. He did, however, resolve to help if the chance ever came.

'What happened to the plan to let Edrich concentrate on the second team leadership?' asked John Kay. Edrich, he said, had done a magnificent job in preparing such players as Pullar, Marner and Barber for stardom; then with dramatic suddenness had come his dismissal. 'The plain truth,' he wrote, 'lay in the fact that Edrich refused to name one or two of his young charges who had indulged in some high-spirited junketing on a second team trip. He accepted full responsibility, as all good captains should – and paid the price . . .

'It was one of the many tragedies of Lancashire cricket that Geoffrey Edrich was not allowed to complete the job he set out to do at Old Trafford.'

Mostly John

From the very first day that John appeared in the nets at the Oval, even before his National Service, he attracted criticism, and over his career he was to become an even more controversial cricketer than Bill. The first-team nets were on one side of the ground, the second-team nets on the other, and the established players, knowing that John would be having his first knock that morning, watched for him to pad up, and some of them strolled over. There was a steady stream of adverse comment about his methods and technique. 'Look at the way he played that one!' 'He'll never made the grade playing like that!' But after a few minutes Bernard Constable, the senior player amongst those watching, said quietly: 'I've noticed one thing – he hasn't missed one yet.'

John had not gone short of cricket – or runs – in the Army, and he had played nine or ten games a season for Surrey II; but in three appearances for the Combined Services he had failed dismally. Two of these games, one each in 1956 and 1957, had been against his own county at the Oval, when he particularly wanted to do well; but in the first of them he got a 'pair', clean bowled each time, and in the second he made 7 and 0, confirming the majority opinion. Nevertheless when he returned to the Oval for his second full season in 1958 he did so well for the Seconds that he was given a first-team chance in the last match, against Worcestershire. Surrey had already won their seventh successive championship, and this gave them a chance to blood a new player.

The match was interrupted by rain, the second day being

washed out entirely; and on the third day, with John, as next man in, waiting with his pads on, Alec Bedser declared 120 behind. Worcestershire responded by declaring at 54 for five, leaving Surrey to get 175 in 130 minutes, but a sporting wicket made the task difficult. 'Apart from John Edrich,' said *Wisden,* 'no one batted confidently,' and Surrey were shot out for 57. John, with 24 not out, was easily top scorer, and only one other player reached double figures. It was a chastening moment for the capped Surrey players.

John's first innings for Surrey thus came on 5th September 1958. Bill had played his last innings for Middlesex just over a fortnight earlier, curiously enough against Surrey. Like Bradman he finished in poignant fashion – caught sub. bowled Laker, 0. Geoffrey had played his last first-class match two months earlier, so the Edrich continuity was only just maintained.

None of the four Edrich brothers had gone out on a high note. But if there was anti-climax in their departures, it was soon forgotten in the early weeks of the 1959 season in the spectacular baptism of cousin John.

National Service had done a lot to mature the raw Norfolk youth who had first reported to the Oval three years earlier. He was less sensitive about his Norfolk accent, and he understood a little better the continual ribbing and micky-taking which was the staple dressing-room badinage. He lacked the sharp Cockney wit that would have enabled him to give as good as he got, but he learned how to take it. He knew they criticised his methods, and he knew too that he was a clumsy fielder and an excruciatingly bad net bowler; but for Club and Ground and Second XI he kept on getting runs, and that was the most silencing riposte of all.

After leaving him out of the first four matches, Surrey introduced him into the side at Trent Bridge in the middle of May – but only because of injuries to other players. As he went in to bat on that Saturday with Micky Stewart he was so palpably nervous that Stewart offered him a few words of advice. 'You've got a good wicket to bat on here,' he said, 'all you've got to do is play as you've always played and you'll get runs.'

Cotton and Davison opened the bowling, with Jepson first change, and the runs had to be fought for. After an hour's batting the score was 39. Stewart was caught at 46, and Barrington 20 runs later, but then came a long stand with the percipient Constable. After three hours fifty minutes, with Mike Willett as his partner, John reached his maiden first-class century in his second Championship match.

Despite the short back-lift which was always to be characteristic of him, and which Andy Sandham, the Surrey coach, had tried to improve in vain, he seemed to get tremendous power when he went for his shots. It came mostly from his strength of forearm, which also enabled him to use an abnormally heavy bat. 'I know of no other English cricketer who uses so heavy a bat as Edrich,' says Brian Close. Tall for an Edrich – he was five feet eight – he was also sturdily built.

Surrey's lead on first innings in this match was only 21, so when they batted again they needed runs. This time John found the going easier, and when he got into the thirties Ken Barrington told him between overs: 'You can get another hundred here if you try.'

In a career lasting twenty-five years, Bill had never got a hundred in each innings. Now John proceeded to do it right at the start of his career.

It was the beginning of the most phenomenal start any batsman has ever had in first-class cricket. In his first seven innings that season he made four hundreds, and he scored 774 runs in his first month. In 25 innings, including the one in 1958, he made 1,291 runs at an average of 71, and by mid-July he was playing at Lord's for the Players against the Gentlemen, an honour that had never come the way of his distinguished coach. But there the recognition ended.

'Morning lad – we haven't seen you before, have we?' This was Freddy Trueman's opening gambit when they met for the first time, the intention being to put him at a psychological disadvantage. But he proceeded to put on 150 with Ken Barrington for the second wicket. The second meeting, however, did not go so well. On a lively pitch, Trueman got the ball to rear nastily off a length, and the result for John was a badly bruised base knuckle of the index finger, and a visit to Bradford Infirmary, where the fracture that everyone suspected was confirmed. This put him out of the game for nearly a month, robbing him of the chance he seemed to have of playing for England before the summer was out. But this chance was more apparent than real, as his name was not included in the long list of twenty-nine 'possibles' issued by the MCC for the West Indies tour that winter.

For a young man of twenty-one to score as heavily and consistently as John had done, to be chosen to represent the Players, and then to be ignored when it came to a major tour, seemed incomprehensible to many; John certainly found it so. It was the first of many unaccountable snubs that he was to suffer at the hands of the England selectors.

The seeds of doubt about his class had already been insidiously sown. 'The success of Edrich, a young left-hander, was astonishing,' said *Wisden*; but for many the remark had a double meaning. Even amongst the Surrey players there remained the feeling that his style and method could not possibly produce such figures over a long period. He played and missed with horrifying frequency for a top-class batsman, and if every catch that he had offered that year had been taken his figures would certainly have been less spectacular.

For the selectors, whose habit was to look for the 'class' player, and who were interested not only in the volume of runs but also in how they were made, he was too uncertain a prospect as yet. 'The selectors, no doubt wisely,' said *Wisden*, 'preferred not to promote him too soon.' But however that may be, a second injury to the same knuckle made all such speculation academic, and that winter the ubiquitous Bill Tucker removed a piece of bone from his leg to remake the knuckle joint. The finger was thicker than before, but it did not hamper him in any way.

In 1959, after seven years at the top, Surrey had been pegged back to equal second, and in 1960, when Laker retired and May was still recuperating from an operation, they were never serious contenders for the championship. But one of the delights of the season was the opening partnership of Stewart and Edrich, their contrasting styles – artist and artisan, one writer called them, a superficial view which nevertheless had its points – and their running between the wickets being always worth watching. They headed the Surrey batting, shared ten hundreds equally, and looked a certain England opening pair of the future. But so far as John was concerned there were two left-handers, Pullar and Subba Row, barring the way.

The man who saw most of John at the wicket in that 1960 season was naturally Micky Stewart, and he remembers how John seemed to be improving all the time, and to be playing and missing far less frequently, though still too often for the purists. The majority of bowlers in any period are right-handed, and this presents any left-hander with the continual problem of the ball slanting across the bat. One has only to remember how many good players have been confounded by left-arm bowlers like Davidson and Sobers, setting very similar problems to the right-hander, to understand the dilemma. It was a weakness that John would always have to contend with, and never perhaps completely eliminate; but in his own way he was working it out.

After an erratic start to the 1961 season, and two failures in the first Surrey match against the Australians, John had a solid run of big scores leading up to the first Test. There was a doubt about Ted Dexter's fitness, and en route from Northampto to Taunton to play Somerset, a message reached him that he was wanted to stand by.

Thus after only two seasons of first-class cricket, John was in line for a cap against Australia. But Dexter was passed fit, and it was John who was incapacitated when he fell ill with tonsilitis soon after. He then missed several matches through injury, got a 'pair' in the second Surrey match against the Australians in August, and finished the season disappointingly. The hundred he got against the Australians at Scarborough in September was little consolation since the game was played in a light-hearted, festival manner, with batsmen given one to get off the mark, no lbw appeals, and no defensive fields; and he was not unduly surprised when he failed to find a place in the India/Pakistan tour that winter.

Bill's impact on Norfolk cricket was immediate; from seventh from bottom of the twenty-eight minor counties involved in 1958, he lifted them to seventh from the top. For far too many years, Norfolk had given blood transfusions to distant counties, suffering anaemia herself in the process. Now here was the prodigal's return, and that is how Bill was greeted wherever he went. In many respects he revolutionised the whole outlook of county cricket in Norfolk, for whereas the idea in the past had often been to build up big scores and attempt to bowl the opposition out twice, Bill's policy, as with Middlesex, was always to leave the door open. And now that he was relieved of the inhibitions inseparable from the handling of men who were playing cricket for a living, he was able to give a policy of challenging, dynamic, do-or-die cricket full rein. He insisted on a result at any price, shunned the struggle for first innings points whenever he could, and kept the over rate up to 22 an hour despite a preponderance of faster bowlers. Some of the old hands, Michael Falcon among them, were inclined to think he was cheapening the second-class game; but the results, and the interest that one exciting finish after another aroused, soon won the doubters over.

Bill averaged 46 with the bat in that first season, and in 153 overs of off-spin took 19 wickets at 20 runs each. And his second season was an outstanding one – 853 runs, average 53, and 43 wickets at an average of 16. Norfolk won six of their ten matches and topped the Minor Counties table, and that they lost the Challenge Match against Lancashire II was a tragedy for them. Yet it was a belated triumph for another Edrich, who had brought on most of the batsmen on the winning side, and whose old colleagues, Tattersall and Hilton, were among the successful bowlers.

Thrown out of work so abruptly in mid-1959 when it was far too late to fix anything for that year, Geoffrey had gone home to Norfolk in the depths of a depression that would have utterly destroyed a lesser man. Indeed, but for Olga and the children he could hardly have fought back. Olga's hairdressing business saved them financially, however, and for the summer of 1960 Geoffrey looked to the Leagues. He answered an advertisement for a professional to Workington, in the North Lancashire League, and he was offered a three-year contract, which he accepted. Too honest to pretend that he liked Workington, he nevertheless buckled down to the job and gave of his best.

Something of what he was up against is suggested by a report of his first game for his new club. Having dismissed their opponents for 97, Workington passed their score with five wickets down, Geoffrey completing his fifty with the last stroke of the match. This landmark guaranteed him a collection; but 'by that time there were few spectators left on the ground'. The Workington club, however, authorised a collection at the next home game.

There were few big names in the North Lancashire League, and Geoffrey topped the League averages easily enough. He also played twelve innings for Cumberland in the Minor Counties competition and topped their averages as well. Back at Old Trafford against Lancashire II, he made 47 and 52 in a great game which Cumberland lost in the penultimate over, and he felt that to some extent he had laid the Old Trafford ghost. Malcolm Hilton got him in the first innings, Roy Tattersall in the second; but he could not have had a more affectionate welcome.

In his second year he topped the League averages again and came second for Cumberland. But for all the kindness that they met, neither he nor Olga could altogether forget the past, and Geoffrey at this time was never fully fit. One man, however, had not forgotten his promise: Geoffrey Howard. When the appointment of groundsman/coach at Cheltenham College was advertised, Howard urged Geoffrey's claims. 'I should forget all about what happened at Old Trafford,' he advised them. 'It's irrelevant – and you won't get a more dedicated man.'

He got the job, and Workington Cricket Club agreed to

release him. 'I wish to say how greatly we all admired him,' said the club secretary before he left, 'not only for his ability as a cricketer, but for the great example he has set to all our players.' To know that he had been appreciated made this chapter of his life more than tolerable after all. Now a new chapter was opening, and he and Olga looked forward to it with keen anticipation. They soon settled down, and they learned to love Cheltenham; but there were still times when the memory of the wrong done to them at Old Trafford haunted them.

With the return of Peter May to regular first-class cricket in 1962, the Surrey batting order was as strong as any in the country. Stewart got 2,000 runs and played twice for England against Pakistan, John narrowly missed getting 2,500, and with May and Barrington at Nos. 3 and 4, and a rejuvenated Constable following a knee-cap operation at No. 5, runs were plentiful. Surrey were once again serious contenders for the championship, and one of their best wins was at Trent Bridge, where John made 216, his first double-century, and took his aggregate on that ground to 700 in seven innings. The top ten batsmen in the country that year were Simpson, Graveney, Dexter, Cowdrey, May, Edrich, Barrington, Parfitt, Stewart and Sheppard, and in a year when the selectors were paying lip-service to fielding as the decisive quality, Stewart was even unluckier not to go to Australia that winter than John.

The game that settled it was the Gentlemen v. Players match at Lord's in July, when Stewart failed twice and Sheppard made a come-back with a 'class' hundred. A second innings of 77 not out from John, in the course of which he put on 118 with Parfitt to win the match, failed to convince the selectors that he was a better prospect as an opener than Pullar, and it was Parfitt who got the remaining place. In Test Trials, which this match had become, it is the first innings that counts.

Writing of the Edrich-Parfitt stand, *Wisden* said : 'These two youngsters pleased a large crowd with their nimble running between the wickets,' and certainly Parfitt was a marvellous runner and a better field than John. But at twenty-five they were hardly youngsters. The time for them both had surely come. Yet John himself did not disagree with the selectors. He did not think he was ready. And in the following summer, against the West Indies, his view was to some extent confirmed.

To judge performance on figures alone, though, is often a mistake. In that series, England's opening batsmen were up against Hall and Griffith at their fastest, not to mention Sobers, and it is not surprising that only two fifty partnerships for the first wicket resulted. John, as it happened, was concerned in both.

When John was chosen with his Surrey partner to open in the first Test, the two batsmen were promised a run of three matches. But the promise was not kept. Yet they began well. When the West Indies declared at 501 for six on the second day at Manchester, they faced Hall and Griffith at their most menacing. That they were erratic as well was equally unsettling. 'To their credit Stewart and Edrich did not falter,' said *Wisden*. But Hall had John caught behind next morning, and England, dismissed for 205, were obliged to follow on.

With the West Indies pressing for a break-through that evening, the two Surrey players produced England's best opening stand for eight Tests by putting on 93 for the first wicket, and they looked like seeing the third day out when John got himself caught at short leg with three overs to go. 'I could have kicked myself,' he says. Only Stewart played the sort of innings that was required next day, and England went to Lord's one down. Yet the general impression was that they had at last found a worthy opening pair.

'With my first ball in my first Test at Lord's,' wrote Charlie Griffith later, 'I had John Edrich caught behind.' That was the unhappy story, and in the second innings, too, John was caught behind, this time off Hall. The ball did no more than brush his glove, and he might have got away with it had he stayed, but John was always a 'walker'. The manner of these two dismissals, however, and of the first one at Old Trafford – all three caught behind – stirred up all the old prejudices about

John's vulnerability to this kind of delivery. 'When he was dropped,' says Micky Stewart, 'I thought it was a terrible mistake.' He was replaced by Peter Richardson.

Trueman, with twelve for 119, won this Test almost on his own to put England level; but the man chosen to partner Stewart in the fourth and fifth Tests was Bolus. Then, just before the Oval game, with England one down, Stewart was taken ill, and John found himself in the side after all. Thus he took part in the decider, the one England had to win to square the series. Watched by a huge crowd two-thirds of which was West Indian, the game exploded into life on the first morning with a violent new-ball barrage from Hall and Griffith. Stimulated by the loss of the toss, which they feared might be fatal for them on the Oval wicket, these two great fast bowlers gave it all they had.

'We had to split Bolus and Edrich before they bedded down,' says Hall. 'To do that we had to keep them guessing by constantly varying length and direction. Bumpers and yorkers are a legitimate weapon in a pace bowler's armoury. The bouncer is not used to intimidate batsmen – but to dismiss them.' (Here Hall must have had his tongue in his cheek.) 'It is a ball which is extremely difficult to play ... I let go a few screamers ... They curled and spat viciously short of a length.' Bolus and Edrich, thought Hall, did not relish them. Neither did umpire Buller. After John had suffered a painful blow on the elbow, Buller spoke to Worrell. 'We don't want this sort of bowling to get out of hand,' he said, 'otherwise I shall have to speak to the bowler.' Worrell accepted the rebuke.

'The two openers stayed defiant,' continues Wes Hall, 'for an hour and a half.' And by doing so they earned the respect of all who saw them. But then both were caught behind the wicket trying to drive Sobers, and although England got a first innings lead, and the openers survived again for a time, the wicket showed no signs of wear, and in the finish the West Indies won easily, as they thoroughly deserved to do.

In six innings John had scored 103 runs, highest score 38, average 17, so on figures alone he had failed in his first Test series. Ye he had shown immense courage and concentration, and his Surrey partnership with Stewart seemed likely to be carried further in the Test arena. But that old question mark about his 'class' still obscured his real merit. And there was the undeniable weakness around the off stump. In five out of six Test dismissals he had edged a catch to the wicket-keeper.

In 1961 at Lakenham, against Staffordshire (skippered by John Ikin), Bill hit two centuries in a match for the first time in his life. He averaged 79 that year with the bat, and he also topped the bowling averages. In 1962 and 1963 his batting average, by an extraordinary coincidence, was exactly the same – 41.92 – and his off-spinners were more than ever in demand to get sides out. At the age of 47 he was carrying the side. He kept it up in 1964 with over 700 runs at an average of just under 40 and 25 wickets; but after those first two tremendous seasons he was finding it more difficult to manoeuvre his side into a favourable position on the second day. Thus Norfolk as a county did not do so well, partly because the batting was more brittle, partly because the seam bowling was less penetrative, partly because opposing captains showed less readiness to co-operate in attitudes that experience told them often led to their downfall.

The eight-week tour of India that took place at the beginning of 1964 was marred by a crop of illnesses which at one point left the party with ten fit men. The chief sufferer was Micky Stewart, who was eventually flown home, but John missed three Tests through a throat infection. All five Tests were drawn, and if no one exactly improved his reputation, no one irrevocably damaged it either. 'Edrich did not score heavily in his two Test innings,' said *Wisden*, 'but he played well on both occasions.' With Geoffrey Boycott now another strong contender, competition for batting places in the England side against the Australians that summer was going to be keen.

The first five batsmen for the first Test at Nottingham were intended to be Boycott, Edrich, Dexter, Cowdrey and Barrington, which looked England's strongest line-up for years. For his first appearance against Australia, John could not have chosen a more agreeable venue. But for once Trent Bridge proved an unlucky ground for him. Practising in the nets on the afternoon before the game, he trod on the ball and twisted his ankle. Hoping to be all right next morning, he said nothing. When he found he could barely walk, he suffered not only the disappointment of missing the game but also the humiliation of a dressing-down as well. No spare batsman was available, and with men like Stewart and Bolus having fully earned a chance to play against Australia, Titmus opened the innings with Boycott.

What kept him silent, says John, was the memory of that first match against the 1961 Australians, when he had stood by for Dexter and not been wanted. His anxiety not to be disappointed again was perhaps understandable. And with Boycott out of action for the second Test at Lord's, the selectors decided that John had had punishment enough, and they picked him.

The first two days of this Test were washed out, but on the Saturday Dexter put the Australians in and they were bowled out for 176, Trueman taking five for 48. In Boycott's absence Dexter opened the innings with John, but he was yorked almost at once. Cowdrey then joined John and they finished the day at 26 for one.

The intervening Sunday, 21st June, was John's twenty-seventh birthday. It was ten years since he had first played for Norfolk, and six since that 'astonishing' entry into first-class cricket; the delay in his first appearance against the toughest of all opposition had been too long, but it said much for England's batting strength in that period. Next day he proceeded to show the selectors how wrong they had been.

'The fourth day belonged to Edrich,' said *Wisden*. And indeed without him England would have been in desperate trouble. In making 120 of England's modest total of 246 John batted six-and-a-quarter hours, and he got a standing ovation when he was eighth out at 229. 'Edrich has a tough cricketing character,' said John Woodcock of *The Times*. 'He should serve England well for many years.'

Somehow, though, the plaudits fell short when it came to the superlatives. They almost seemed to be grudging, to dismiss him as a plodder who might come in useful in hard times but for whom some more exciting substitute might be found. 'More than once,' wrote John Clarke, 'he looked in great peril.' It was left to an Australian, Jack Fingleton, to appreciate his full value.

> England have found a good left-hander in John Edrich...
> He has a cool, sensible head. He has an odd grip, as it
> seems from a distance, with his bottom hand, and I de-
> tected a gap between his two hands on the handle. The
> theorists wouldn't quite agree with this... but then Don
> Bradman had an unusual grip with his top hand. Good
> players are sometimes a law unto themselves. I liked Edrich
> and his approach to the game. I admire the man who can
> hold tight and get runs when they are most wanted in a
> Test.

That was an Australian view. But although John was credited with having fought hard in the next Test at Leeds to pull the game round his scores were modest, and in the fourth Test at Old Trafford, when both sides got over 600, he followed a rising ball from McKenzie early on and missed out on the mammoth scoring. 'Edrich came back, a pitiful figure,' wrote Clarke; and the selectors, still suspicious of that off-side weakness, took the opportunity to replace him with Barber at the Oval. Then, for all the world as though they were hitting a man when he was down, they left him out of the South African tour that winter. 'If some of his previous exclusions were blunders,' says Micky Stewart, 'this was diabolical.'

For John, what made the omission all the more devastating was that he suspected it might be justified. He knew that he would never attain the classic style of a May, a Cowdrey or a Graveney, still less the arrogance of a Dexter; and he had found that in Test cricket, far more than in the county game, he had to graft for his runs. Was he, perhaps, just a good county player and not much more? And if that were so, what ambitions did he have left? Did he really want to carry on?

It was a time for taking stock. For any first-class cricketer, the opportunities to enjoy life are there for the taking, and from his earliest days at the Oval John had embraced them. 'I used to be a bit of a tearaway,' he once told John Reason in a *Cricketer* interview; and Micky Stewart confirms this. 'I lived in digs,' says John. 'There was nothing to do but stay for a few drinks and then go on to a club. It's not that you get drunk, or anything like that. It's just so time-consuming. It's not healthy, either, standing around in those sort of places when you've been on your feet all day long in any case.' But this had been the pattern of his life in the summer months, and with a first marriage that had broken up and a career that was losing its impetus and direction, he badly needed a new course to steer. At about this time he met an Australian girl, Judith Cowan, whom he was eventually to marry. She shook him out of his depression and made him believe that he still had a future in the game. Had it not been for Judy he might have shirked the struggle.

Seeing himself in a newsreel during that 1964 summer, he was surprised at his girth. One result was that he decided to become teetotal. He had always held, as Bill had done, that a man's habits were his own affair provided he was fit and at his best next morning. He did not change that as a general, liberal outlook, but to himself he applied a more rigorous routine.

As a cricketer John was a curious mixture. He had never been an enthusiastic fielder, and Surrey in any case had tried to turn him into a wicket-keeper. When this didn't work out, he was obliged to make himself proficient in the field. But he hated being in the outfield, and was only happy when he was near the wicket, where he felt much more in the game. Such facets as the theory and the history of the game interested him little, and he did not believe in concerning himself over-much with the idiosyncracies of bowlers or wickets. Coached by Arthur McIntyre as well as by Sandham, he had absorbed what he wanted, and he tended to ignore the rest, while Sandham and McIntyre had been perceptive enough to recognise that he was an instinctive, intuitive player, and they had never tried to force him into a common mould.

John's basic individualism sometimes made him impatient of the day-to-day responsibilities of being part of a team. His temperament was more suited to the personal combat of tennis and golf than to cricket, and his business sense told him that the man who played for himself was the one who made the money if he was good enough. There were even times when it seemed to some of his Surrey colleagues that he took little interest in the game outside his own knock.

In his make-up, then, there seemed to be many of the hallmarks of the selfish cricketer. Yet he was not selfish in the sense that some of the big run-getters have been selfish. Indeed he was not a selfish player at all. He simply set out to lay the foundations on which the rest of the team could build. Most good players, when they get established, tend to hog the strike; or when the ball is flying around at one end, they have a natural facility for staying at the other. John never did these things, as Micky Stewart, who batted with him more than anyone else in this period, will testify.

Surrey's opening pair in the middle sixties were the best in the country, and in an article for *The Cricketer* Colin Cowdrey got John talking about their problems. 'He felt that in a combination such as theirs,' wrote Cowdrey, 'they come to know which types of bowlers are likely to be dangerous to either one of them at any particular time.' And then he quoted John.

A bowler of the Alan Davidson type, left arm over the wicket, such as Carlton Forbes of Nottinghamshire, could be a very serious threat to Micky Stewart early on, as the ball moved across him towards the slips. Here is an opportunity for me to take the bulk of the bowling from that end. There will be just as many occasions when the situation will be reversed. Then again, we try to achieve a situation where one or other is taking the lead. We never know who this is going to be until the innings gets under way. It depends upon form or the bounce of the ball. After a few overs it is clear that one of us is going well and it is up to the other to play a second fiddle role, relinquishing as much of the strike as possible. Sometimes the positions get reversed during the course of an innings. One of us may get off to a good start and then appear to dry up, the initiative passing to the other. I think it is essential that one person should be making the running and be getting as much of the strike as possible.

For all John's genuine dislike of over-theorising, this makes it plain that he thought clearly and positively about the game. No one in any case could have doubted that he knew precisely what he was at; but from 1964 on he developed much more freely his own ideas and perceptions on the game.

In that winter of 1964–65, while the MCC were touring South Africa, John took a coaching appointment out there, and at the same time, playing in South African club cricket, he was improving his own game, playing hard and straight and driving more aggressively than before. And in the 1965 season in England this paid off. Although for him it proved to be a year of extremes, he scored more runs than anyone else in the country, and after being left out of eight successive Tests he forced his way back into the side for the third Test against New Zealand by producing an orgy of run-getting. His last eight innings before his recall brought him 1,001 runs, his scores being 139, 121 not out, 205 not out, 55, 96, 188, 105, and 92. Yet all this was to be eclipsed in the Test Match at Leeds.

For once in his international career he was nervous before the start, and he took half an hour to get off the mark. He himself described it as a spasmodic innings, and he certainly had his quiet periods. Then he would cut loose. Beaten to the hundred by Barrington, with whom he eventually put on 369, he was well ahead of him at the end of the first day with 194 against 152 – a nice illustration of the point he had made to Colin Cowdrey.

Next day, when Barrington was out for 163, he continued to dominate the cricket, and when England declared at 546 for four he had made 310 not out. 'Never in my life had I been timing the ball so well,' he says. Glorious straight hits, often lofted, and perfectly placed drives either side of cover, were his best forcing shots, and he excelled in the cut. 'He scored comparatively little off his legs,' noted John Woodcock, 'and unlike "W.J." he seldom hooked.'

No player who bats for nearly nine hours, as John did in this match (he was on the field throughout), can escape moments of weariness; nor can he bat so long without offering the occasional chance, however difficult, and playing and missing a few times. But even in this innings it seems that John played and missed surprisingly often. Ken Barrington described him as an enigma. 'He seems to have a fantastic knack of playing and missing without getting a touch. I have seen him – even during his great innings at Leeds – play and miss several times without disaster when thoroughly well set and presumably seeing it like a football.'

This was surely one of the most relentless come-backs of all time. And for once it attracted all the superlatives. But this, for John, remained unusual. Unemotional and undemonstrative in public, so that he seemed far more dour and introverted than he really was, he left the field on that first triumphant day with Barrington without a flicker of a smile. No one would have guessed that he had been enjoying himself, and although the enjoyment was certainly there, he did not communicate it. Yet, according to Micky Stewart, a slow, wide, devastating smile was never far away.

That innings, for 1965, was the peak, and it gave great satisfaction to all his admirers, especially to a senior member of the Edrich clan, Uncle George, now sixty-eight, who was recovering in hospital after an operation. When Bill went to see him he was listening to the radio commentary from Leeds. 'The boy's doing well,' he said, 'do you think they'll declare or let him get 300?' Bill thought the innings had done Uncle George even more good than the operation. 'I told him that John would be going to Australia that winter, and that he ought to go out there to see him, and I'm convinced this helped him to recuperate. John of course was selected, and Uncle George went.'

The rough, for John, came a fortnight later in the first Test, at Lord's, against the second touring side of that year, South Africa. After ten scratchy minutes in the first innings he was lbw to Pollock for a duck, and in the second he lost sight of a shortish ball from the same bowler against the pavilion background and took a sickening blow on the temple. 'It was my own fault,' he says. 'He had bowled me a few bouncers and I could see that he was digging this one in too ... I ducked, but it didn't get up that much and I ducked into it.

'I went dizzy. I was going to stay on. I could have done. Looking back, it would be as well if I had done. It's like a car crash. The only way to get your confidence back is to go straight out and drive again ... I should have gone on batting ... I wouldn't have lost my confidence so much.'

Taken to hospital on a stretcher, with visions of losing the chance he'd earned of his first trip to Australia, he was left with nothing worse than a shattering headache. Unfortunately a residual crop of headaches was to continue for a long time.

As with Bill in 1947, the injury marred what was otherwise easily his best season. He missed the next two matches, and then, in eleven more innings for Surrey, he made only 241 runs, average 22. It was not until the last game of the season, at Scarborough against a Rest of the World XI that included Hall, Griffith and Sobers, that he showed anything like his best form. But by that time he already knew he was booked for Australia.

In the course of that 1965 summer John hit forty-nine 6's, a record for an opening batsman. Only Arthur Wellard, who exceeded fifty 6's four times and holds the record with 72, has hit more sixes in a season. This achievement should have erased that old artisan tag for all time; artisans, one would have thought, don't hit that many sixes. But John continued to bat in his own individual method, and the tag persisted.

Before he flew out with the MCC party under Mike Smith John married Judy, who was to join him later for a honeymoon in Australia. The tour itself, as he says himself, was to prove the happiest of his career.

What, at this watershed in John's career, were the fortunes of his four cousins? Bill, still captaining Norfolk, was retaining his form wonderfully well with bat and ball. In Glamorgan, rising costs and decreasing revenue had forced a curtailment of the coaching scheme and Brian had left to take up a coaching appointment at St Edward's School, Oxford. Eric had returned from New Zealand to get married and was chicken-farming in Huntingdonshire, and Geoffrey was still at Cheltenham.

Something had happened to Geoffrey, though, which had made his contentment complete. He had been invited to return to Old Trafford as senior coach. After all that had happened, it was an unbearably poignant moment, assuaging all the pain he had suffered over many years. The Lancashire committee had been big enough to admit that they were wrong, and Geoffrey was more than ready to go half-way to meet them. He did not, for various reasons, finally take the job; but the effect was to remove the cause of a deep-seated sense of resentment and injustice. The book could now be closed.

Boycott, Barber, Edrich, Barrington, Cowdrey; that was England's batting line-up in the 1965–66 series, and except on one occasion it proved equal to all demands. The exception was the fourth Test at Adelaide, where England's preparation was unfortunate. After a tremendous win at Sydney, where Barber got his 185 and John got 103, they lost their inspiration and their edge in the fortnight's holiday cricket which their schedule demanded, and the loss of the fourth Test eventually meant that the series was drawn.

In the State matches John showed what he could do as an attacking batsman, but in the Tests he played a dual role. 'When Boycott and Barber mastered the Australian bowling,' wrote E. M. Wellings, 'he thumped home the advantage and thus scored two successive centuries.' This was in the second and third Tests. 'When they did not, he was in a tangle, but he battled on and invariably sold his wicket dearly.' One would have thought that his results – 375 runs in eight innings, average 46 – would have silenced criticism, but even Wellings could not forbear to refer to his old weakness. 'Seldom can a batsman have played and missed so often, have so often threatened to get out, and yet scored so well in Australia.' John Woodcock agreed. 'If I were to guess how often he played and missed, it might be considered libellous.'

John himself freely admitted it. 'I played and missed frequently,' he says, 'but I have never seen the point of fussing and worrying over this.' The Australians near the wicket, Simpson and Grout especially, set up a chorus of 'oohs' and 'aahs' in an effort to convince him that he must touch one in a minute – 'but I managed to ignore them'. He was in trouble, too, against Simpson's googlies; but he survived. 'If in doubt I played down the line. I have never been in the habit of watching a spinner's hand.' As always, John knew exactly what he was doing. 'I have a suspicion that too close a scrutiny of a bowler's fingers twenty yards away calls for much too rapid a shortening of focus as the ball approaches.'

Most of what John has learned about batting in the course of his career has come on the plumb wickets he has encountered overseas. 'When I started,' he says, 'I was like most left-handers. I couldn't hit a shot off my legs.' And this had been noticeable even in that great innings of 310. But after his Australian tour it was different. 'Now . . . I've learned to work the ball. I had to. Ask any left-hander where he gets out. He gets out caught at the wicket and caught in the slips. The ball is going across you all the time.

'In Australia . . . I thought about this a lot. I decided to go across more than I did . . . As a result, defensively I now know where my off stump is. If anything is wide of me, I'm happy to let it go until I'm in.'

These were some of John's conclusions (as related in his book and to John Reason) at the end of that tour. But it took him a few weeks to apply them successfully when he got home, and after a double failure in the MCC match against the West Indians at Lord's in May, he knew once again what it was to be dropped. With Milburn seizing his chance, and the outstandingly successful return of Tom Graveney, the fight back looked like being a hard one.

At first England seemed to be managing quite nicely without him. But the third and fourth Tests were lost by large margins, and the selectors were forced to take drastic action. They began by appointing a new captain – Brian Close – to succeed Cowdrey, who was dropped in his turn; and Close, as it happened, was a fervent admirer of John. 'Edrich had the batting qualities that Yorkshiremen admire,' he says. 'It is no secret that when I was first brought in to captain England at the Oval in 1966 I insisted on Edrich being in the side.'

Thus John was the man in possession when India and Pakistan came over to play three Tests each in 1967; and if there were any doubts about his form his innings against the Indians at the Oval for Surrey at the end of May should have dispelled them. Surrey lost two wickets cheaply, and John went cautiously to his fifty, but he then straight drove Bedi three times into the pavilion seats and doubled his score in 65 minutes. Yet after failing in the first two Tests he was again dropped, this time for the rest of the season.

John passed his thirtieth birthday in June of that year, and his career had clearly reached another crisis. Season after season he had been one of the heaviest run-getters in the game, consistently near the top of the averages, and his Test record was an enviable one. Yet he had only to suffer a failure or two at Test level and his foibles were remembered and his merits forgotten. In moments of national discouragement and defeat, as at the Oval in 1966, his qualities were in demand, but for long periods the better-looking player was preferred.

It was natural that the selectors should clutch at an exciting player like Milburn for the West Indian tour. But they were wise enough to take along someone a little less flamboyant as an insurance. Having missed four successive Tests, John was a surprise selection, and even Brian Close thought he was lucky to go. 'Technique is not good,' he wrote in a pen-picture, 'but has an exceptionally good eye and hits the ball with great power, despite having such a short back-lift . . . I once asked him how he developed his strength and he told me : "Pulling up sugar-beet on the farm when I was a boy".'

Instead of being the reserve batsman, as he himself had confidently expected, John became one of the key players. The chance came through Milburn's failure to acclimatise, although his own start, in the words of E. M. Wellings, was 'horrible'. He fell cheaply 'time after time as he dabbed and snicked', and Wellings concluded that the obvious flaws in his batting method were catching up with him. Yet, under Cowdrey's tutelage, he tackled and conquered them, schooling himself yet again to play straighter, and closer to his legs. The result was that he found his form in time for the Tests.

Hall and Griffith still bowled their quota of bumpers in this series, but John showed no sign that the blow from Pollock two-and-a-half years earlier was on his mind, and until the final Test, when he was beaten twice around the off stump by Sobers, he always weathered these storms. His 96 at Kingston, while Cowdrey played the anchor role at the other end, was 'a boldly pugnacious innings' (*Wisden*), which would probably have led to victory but for the bottle-throwing that punctured the tension, and then in the third Test it was his turn to play the innings that held the side together – 146 in seven hours fifty minutes. When the Australians visited England in the summer of 1968 he found himself for the first time an automatic choice.

'He was now the complete player,' recalls Micky Stewart. 'He didn't play and miss any more than any other opening batsman, he hardly edged the ball at all, and above all he knew which ball to leave alone.'

His figures that year fully confirmed Stewart's opinion. Fourth in the averages, with only Boycott, Barry Richards and Kanhai ahead of him, he was one of only three players to reach 2,000 runs. But most convincing of all was his form against Australia.

His scores in the first four Tests were 49 (run out) and 38 at Old Trafford; 7 at Lord's, when he was caught off his gloves trying to fend off a vicious bouncer from McKenzie; 88 and 64 at Edgbaston; 62 and 55 at Headingley; and then, to crown it all, he held the batting together on the first day of the final Test at the Oval with 130 not out, finishing up with 164.

This was a historic game, full of drama from the first, the equal of anything in the long saga of Oval Tests. England, fighting to square the series, were precariously poised at 113 for three on the first day when Graveney joined John. They put on 125 (Graveney 63), and then in came D'Oliviera to play the innings which forced his selection for South Africa that winter – and triggered off the cancellation of the tour.

That innings took John within 25 runs of Compton's record aggregate for an England batsman in a home series against Australia – 562 in 1948; and had the orders not been to fling the bat in England's second innings, he must have set up a new record. As it was he was caught trying to drive Mallett when eight runs short. Then came England's declaration, and an incredible victory with six minutes to spare after a storm had flooded the ground.

Detailed descriptions of most of John's innings are hard to come by; but no one who saw his 164 will forget it. Perhaps the most memorable shots were those hearty clumps through the covers off the back foot; but he never looked in trouble, and the whole innings was entirely devoid of the uncertainties that had sometimes plagued him. 'The more exciting batsmen – Milburn, Dexter and Cowdrey – were out for 45 between them,' wrote John Arlott. 'But John Edrich, the artisan, stayed.' It is not too much to say that the Oval crowd fully expected it of him.

The Australian tour coincided with his benefit year, and although it was not the greatest of summers, he was more than £10,000 better off at the end of it. He was thus the only Edrich to get a really substantial sum. Bill had missed the chance of a similar tax-free benefit by turning amateur, Geoffrey had been unlucky, and Eric and Brian had not qualified for benefits at all. It is probable that John was a better business man than any of them; but to reach his absolute peak in his benefit year was wonderfully fortuitous.

Not the least remarkable feature of the 1960s was the way in which Bill retained his form with bat and ball. And although in 1969 he gave up the captaincy, he remained Norfolk's most successful all-rounder, and in his last full season (1970, at the age of fifty-four), he topped the batting with an average of 35 and was second in the bowling, sending down 238 overs of off-spin and taking 25 wickets at 19 runs each. He appeared only two or three times in 1971, but by doing so he completed forty years in first-class and minor counties cricket – not by any means a record, but a remarkable achievement nevertheless. He scored 8,308 runs for Norfolk, including ten centuries, average 35, and took 417 wickets at 19 runs each.

When Brian took the job at St Edward's School he played his cricket for Buckingham Town, the club he had played for in 1940, 1941 and 1946. Then in 1966, having taken on more responsibilities at the school, he moved house to Oxford, where he was at once asked to play for the county. When school duties permitted he did so, and in four matches that season he scored 329 runs, including two centuries. He was then forty-four; and by topping the Minor Counties averages he carried off the Wilfred Rhodes Trophy. 'Why didn't you play for us when you were playing for Buckingham?' asked the aggrieved players of that county. 'You didn't ask me,' said Brian.

'I was lucky to win the Trophy on the basis of eight innings,' he says. But he had satisfied the qualification terms, and he had certainly made the runs. He had another good season for Oxfordshire in 1967, finishing second in their averages this time, but he was not able to play so much in 1968, and after that he dropped out. Nevertheless this late flowering made a pleasurable end to his career.

In the winter of 1968–69, John went to Ceylon and Pakistan with the MCC; but although he scored more runs than anyone

156

else on the tour, his record in the three Tests against Pakistan was a modest one. In the summer of 1969, however, when the season was split between the West Indians and the New Zealanders, he topped the English averages for the first time, at a fraction under 70 runs per innings. He was the only man to get 2,000 runs that year, and he also topped the overall Test averages with 545 runs, average 54.

Surrey, finishing third, challenged strongly for the championship, failing only because most of their batsmen, according to *Wisden*, somehow exhausted their ration of runs. But they added: 'With the glorious exception of Edrich'. At last John was earning the kind of praise he deserved as England's leading batsman, and at the Oval in mid-July he showed what he could do on a wicket taking spin against Fred Titmus. His 102 not out, said *Wisden*, was 'a sterling innings'. Nobody else shaped with any confidence, and in the fourth innings Middlesex were easily destroyed.

For much of the following season John was troubled by a badly bruised finger, and he did not have quite such a dominating year as in 1969. He was even left out of three of the matches in the Rest of the World series. But when the party was selected to tour Australia that winter under Ray Illingworth he was an automatic choice.

England's success in bringing home the Ashes in 1970–71 was based on Illingworth's leadership, the batting of Boycott, Edrich and Luckhurst, the bowling of Snow and the wicketkeeping of Knott. But if Boycott emerged as the batsman of the series, John was not far behind.

His 79 in England's only innings in the first Test was top score. In the second Test he ran himself out for 47, but he got 115 not out in the second innings, when all around him the batting was weak and the batsmen were puzzled by Gleeson's spin. Had it not been for John, England would certainly have lost.

After the third Test had been washed out, he made 55 and 12 (run out by Boycott) in the fourth, though Boycott's batting, with Snow's bowling, won the match to put England one up. In the fifth Test he and Boycott put on 161 without being separated to draw the match, and in the sixth, with Luckhurst absent, he opened twice with Boycott and put on 107 and 103 – three century opening partnerships in succession, with Dennis Lillee one of the opening bowlers each time. John got a hundred in the first innings of this match and Boycott in the second.

Finally, in the seventh Test, opening with Luckhurst this time because Boycott was absent, he made 30 and 57 in a low-scoring game which England won by 62 runs. If they had lost this match, as for a long time they seemed likely to do, the series would have been halved and they would not have regained the Ashes. John's match aggregate of 87 was higher than anyone else's except Greg Chappell's (95). The decisive stand was the 94 for the first wicket that John put on with Luckhurst in the second innings after England had been overtaken by 80 runs on the first.

648 runs in the six-match series (which was what it amounted to), put him second only to Boycott. Boycott's average of 92 was the second highest by an England batsman in a Test series in Australia after Hammond, and only three other men – Hobbs, Hutton and Sutcliffe – have bettered John's figures.

Returning to an English home season on this pinnacle of achievement, John was a key member of Surrey's 1971 championship-winning side. Despite his many absences on duty for England, against either Pakistan or India (he missed eleven championship matches), he scored 1,718 runs for Surrey, including six hundreds. This makes all the more puzzling his results that year in the Tests. Only once, in the second Test against India at Lord's in July, did he really excel; but then 'a doughty 62 by Edrich prevented another England collapse against the spinners' (*Wisden*) and certainly saved the game. The long and arduous Australian tour, perhaps, had taken the edge off his performance at the highest level, and several other steady displays could not camouflage a disappointing Test record – 267 runs in eleven innings, average 24.

There were other things on his mind, too. One of them was

the captaincy of Surrey. Half-way through that 1971 season Stewart announced his resignation as captain. His leadership, although sometimes criticised, had been dedicated and unselfish, and he wanted to end his career with a season or two free from the cares and responsibilities he had carried for the past nine years. The Surrey committee urged him to reconsider, and it was with considerable reluctance that he finally acquiesced. He had clearly earned the break for which he had asked. Why had the committee talked him into continuing? It could only be because they were worried about the succession.

1972 was the year of Dennis Lillee versus Dad's Army, as Illingworth's ageing team was discourteously called. Lillee took 31 wickets in the series, setting up a new record for an Australian in England, but the old-timers managed to hold on to retain the Ashes.

Between the first and second Tests John had his thirty-fifth birthday – old by Australian standards, but not by England's. And for Surrey that year he proved as dependable as ever. He began the season with two model centuries at Lord's, one against the MCC for Surrey and one against the Australians for the MCC, and he played well in the first Test at Old Trafford before running himself out at 49. Had he known then that he would not get a single fifty in the entire series he might have been more cautious.

So many times in Australia he had been the rock on which the England innings was built. Now, although he played several valuable innings, he could not get beyond the thirties and forties. He failed completely at Lord's in Massie's match, though the way the right-handers played and missed – or played and edged – at the ball slanted across the body must have afforded him a certain grim amusement. His 37 in the first innings at Trent Bridge was top score, and he was the only England batsman to cope on the spinner's wicket which confounded the Australians at Leeds. But in the final Test Lillee got him cheaply twice, and in ten Test Match innings he averaged only 21.

His Test record since returning from the 1970–71 tour of

Australia read: o and 15, 37, 2 and 33, 18 and 62, o and 59, 41 and o; 49 and 26, 10 and 6, 37 and 15, 45 and 4, and 8 and 18. England's batting had been badly shaken up by the speed of Lillee that summer, and for the tour of India and Pakistan that winter the selectors were forced to rebuild. John, in fact, withdrew his name from the list of possibles 'for business reasons'; but his absence from the touring party went unremarked.

When the New Zealanders and West Indians toured England in 1973, John was not even scoring heavily for Surrey. After ten years in which the selectors had seemed unable to make up their minds about him, they had finally stuck with him to the bitter end. Nothing seemed more certain now than that he had played his last Test Match.

Despite their championship win in 1971, it had not been a happy season internally for Surrey, and at the end of it Bob Willis left for Warwickshire. Stewart, having been persuaded to carry on in 1972 as captain, must have wished the committee had let him have his way, as he could not strike any sort of form and played in only thirteen championship matches. John was frequently away playing against Australia, and Surrey were often led in Stewart's absence by wicket-keeper Arnold Long. This third-string role was one he had frequently played in the past, and it now seemed that he was being groomed to take over from Stewart.

With Stewart's retirement, the dilemma that Surrey had tried to postpone was upon them. The natural successor to Stewart was John. But the heir apparent seemed to be Long. Yet if John wanted the captaincy, it would be a delicate matter preferring someone else.

John's contented domestic life, which had been such an important factor in his achievement of world rank as a batsman, militated against him in some ways when it came to leadership of a county side. If he was playing at the Oval, he tended to go straight home when the day's play was over. He didn't often stop any length of time for a drink and a chat with the boys.

Vintage 1975; a straight drive
off Phil Carrick at the Oval
against Yorkshire . . .

. . . and a pull for 4 off Ashley
Mallett on the way to 175 in the
Lord's Test against Australia

'Cricket will have to give *me* up.' Bill batting in a charity match in 1975; *below,* the cricketing family Edrich in 1967, showing Bill senior and Edith centre, and Edwin, the first Edrich to play for Norfolk, second from left in the front row

His attitude to the game, his involvement with other players, and his ability to communicate, had improved enormously as he matured, but he remained an individualist. And it was fully expected at that time that he would continue to miss many matches through Test calls.

The man who is the England player may find it difficult not to appear a man apart. Cyril Washbrook had had this problem at Old Trafford. But when John made it plain that he wanted the job, that it was his ambition to 'do something for Surrey', and that he would certainly react to being passed over, the Surrey committee duly appointed him.

As it happened, in that first season under his captaincy, he was not absent on Test duties at all, which helped a good deal. But he did miss several matches through a troublesome leg injury, which hampered him at times even when he played. The result was a moderate season – 1,069 runs, average 34. Many county batsmen would have been well satisfied with such a record, but not John; apart from 1961, when his average was marginally less, it was his worst since he started in first-class cricket fourteen years earlier. Younis and Roope were the leading Surrey batsmen, and John was sixth in the county averages.

John had given the matter of captaincy a good deal of thought before he took over. He knew that he must aim at establishing his authority at once, that he must play it his way, and that he must earn the confidence of the team, so that they accepted that everything he did was for the benefit of the side as a whole. But he could hardly have taken over at a more difficult time. After ten years under one captain the team had inevitably got into a groove, and some of the senior players could be expected to resent any attempt to jog them out of it. Despite the triumph of 1971, the dominant characteristic of those years had been frustration – frustration with results that everyone, Stewart included, felt ought to have been so much better with the talent available. John, as dedicated a cricketer as any of his cousins, felt there were times when not every man in the side was pulling his weight. So it is not surprising that, in his first season as captain, the side was still not a happy one.

Even amongst John's opponents there was a feeling at first that his methods were inclined to be flat and uninspired. But it was characteristic of him to go about the job quietly. And in that first season under his leadership Surrey produced a remarkable late rally that took them to second place in the table. Thus when, in the autumn of 1973, a faction amongst the playing staff called for a new leader, the committee stood by John. Had they not done so, it is very likely that he would have retired from first-class cricket.

Captaining Surrey looked like being his final distinction in the game. If that were denied him, what other ambitions did he have? He had lost his place in the England side, and the road back looked impossibly hard. It was highly uncharacteristic for an Edrich to shirk a challenge, but at thirty-six one had to be realistic. He no longer had the zest for such a struggle.

Whatever he lacked, though, it wasn't courage. Mistakes in his first season had been inevitable, and he knew there had been times when his popularity rating was low. But that tremendous late run had showed what the side could do. He would finish the job he had started.

After playing three Tests against the West Indies towards the end of that summer, England went out to the Caribbean to play five more Tests against the same opponents. The exclusion of John Edrich aroused no comment whatsoever.

What had caused John's loss of form? 'Within a year or two of the start of the Sunday League in 1969,' says Micky Stewart, 'with its pressures on batsmen to run the ball down through the vacant slip area, John had become liable to slip back into bad habits, even in the three-day game. I think this had a lot to do with his relative lack of success.' But in this John was no different from scores of other county batsman. And this was soon to become apparent.

The failure of Jameson and Hayes in the West Indies, the moderate form of Mike Denness, and the absence of any obvious successors, inclined the selectors, when they came to choose the sides for the Test Trial in May 1974, to look for stability to reinforce the success of Amiss and Fletcher. Looking back, they could not help but remember the inept display of English batting against Indian spin in 1972–73. Perhaps a left-hander might counter it. Looking forward, they had to bear in mind the Australian tour that was due to take place that winter.

That tour of India and Pakistan was the one from which John had opted out. But he had now had a summer and two winters' rest from Test cricket, he felt much better in himself, and his attitude was different. He knew what the presence of senior players like Tom Graveney, Ken Barrington and Colin Cowdrey had meant to his own early Test career, and he had come to believe that two or three senior men were especially valuable on tour to help the younger players. This, he felt, after going out to watch the third Test that winter in Barbados, had been missing in the West Indies, where there were no elder statesmen.

He made no secret of his ambition to tour Australia a third time. But could he come back at thirty-seven? Bill had done it, so why not John? That, perhaps, was the selectors' attitude. With six Tests in front of them that summer, they had plenty of room for manoeuvre, and they chose John to open for The Rest against England in the Trial. He responded by getting 106 out of 267 for eight declared in the first innings and 95 out of 142 for three in the second, and after missing 19 matches he was back in the side for the first Test against India at Old Trafford.

After failing in the first innings, John made a hundred in the second 'with very little trouble', according to John Woodcock. 'The fourth day belonged to Edrich,' said *Wisden*. 'He returned to the scene rejuvenated.' He played in all six Tests that summer, and at last his batting met with unqualified approval. 'Batted in a cool, confident manner'; 'timed his strokes perfectly'; 'confidently saw England to the close'; 'the revival was inspired by Edrich' : these were some of the endorsements signed by *Wisden*. He became an automatic choice for Australia.

When the time came he was appointed vice-captain under Mike Denness, confirming rumours that he had been seriously considered for the captaincy itself. And there were forecasts that, if Denness's form was as disappointing as some people were predicting, he might in fact find himself captaining England against Australia. If that happened, what sort of captain would he make?

The Surrey committee had not been the only ones to doubt his potential as a leader. 'I must confess that when Edrich was first appointed to succeed Stewart,' wrote Richard Streeton in *The Cricketer*, 'I wondered if he would find the task too onerous. He has, in fact, made a howling success of it . . . The going was initially hard in 1973, I suspect. The sheer character of the man inevitably won through.' It did so to such an extent that, following that dramatic late run for the championship in 1973, Surrey in 1974 won the Benson and Hedges Cup.

'It was round Edrich's chunky frame that the entire edifice was triumphantly erected,' wrote Streeton. 'All the main virtues of both Edrich himself and those of his team were epitomised time and time again along the Benson roadway.' In April, against Sussex, 'it was Edrich who personally held off the potential threat from John Snow's pace . . . Two good catches and some shrewd captaincy touches completed Edrich's claim to the Gold Award. Two more performances in the same ilk later again brought Edrich the Gold Award in the semi-final round and final.' In the final, against Leicestershire, billed as 'Illy against Edie', John's captaincy did not suffer by comparison. 'Amid all this striving and endeavour,' concluded Streeton, 'Edrich was at the same time re-capturing his own Test place. Truly a wonderful summer for him.'

If there was anything wrong with that 1974 summer, it was that one-day cricket, India, and even Pakistan, were hardly adequate preparation for Australia. Batting against Lillee and Thomson on the wickets that were prevalent that winter belonged to another world. 'Dear Mum,' one of the MCC tourists is reputed to have written in a letter home, 'I got a half-volley the other day – in the nets.' Christopher Martin-Jenkins has suggested that John might have been happier at home with his family than far away in Australia risking life and limb. 'Yet, of course, when he is faced with a challenge and courage more than anything else is required, Edrich, though he will feign reluctance, will be the last person in the world to stop fighting.' And so it proved.

In the first Test at Brisbane, Australia batted first and made 309, and England were 9 for one on the second day when John went to the wicket. Soon they were 57 for four, with Amiss, Luckhurst, Denness and Fletcher out. Greig then joined John in England's only real stand of the match, and at close of play England were 114 for four, John not out 40, Greig not out 34. Once again John had held England together, and in the course of this innings he passed 2,000 runs in Tests against Australia. Of post-war English cricketers only Hutton, Compton and Barrington have achieved this feat.

John was out next morning for 48, but Greig made 110, and England finished only 44 behind on first innings. Then came utter disaster: Australia 288 for five declared, England all out 166. John bruised a hand so badly in this innings that he missed the second Test at Perth, as did Amiss and Lloyd with broken fingers, evidence of how fiercely the ball was lifting. Cowdrey was flown out in an attempt to fill the gap.

After England had lost the second Test by nine wickets, Amiss and Lloyd returned to the side with John for the third Test at Melbourne. Once again John held the side together after a disastrous start, this time with Cowdrey, and his 49 was top score among the batsmen, only Knott exceeding it with 52. In the second innings Amiss played his only substantial innings of the series, and John failed; but England escaped defeat. Nevertheless they went into the fourth Test at Sydney two down, knowing that if they lost it they must surrender the Ashes. It was in this situation that Denness asked to be left out and the captaincy passed to John.

To captain England against Australia must surely be the summit of every cricketer's ambition. Now, against all reasonable expectation a year or so back, John had achieved it. But it was an unenviable succession. Throughout the tour John, as heir apparent, had kept a low profile, giving full support to the much-criticised Denness. Now the responsibility for recovering the lost ground rested with him.

The assumption was that if Denness regained any sort of form he would return for the fifth Test. So John could only regard himself as a caretaker captain. England could still hang on to the Ashes if they could draw this match and win the last two, unlikely as that seemed; and by the time Australia had batted and made 405, a draw was the best England could hope for.

'The chance to see Thomson and Lillee at full steam, with the Poms on the run, is proving Australia's greatest summer attraction,' wrote John Woodcock; and over the five days 178,000 people turned up to see the England batsmen pounded, pummelled and pulverised into submission. Of the first six batsmen John was easily top scorer with 50, and only a typical 82 from Knott saved the follow on. On a pitch that was still good Australia took no chances, and England were eventually set 400 to win.

When two hours were lost to rain on the fourth afternoon, England only had to battle it out through the last day, with all their wickets intact when they started, to save the game and, for the moment, the Ashes.

At 42 for two, with Lloyd and Cowdrey out, John joined Amiss. This was a bad enough start, but worse was to come. Time and again Thomson and Lillee had been warned for the persistent bowling of bouncers, but now, as John faced up to his first ball from Lillee, he made exactly the same mistake he had made against Pollock ten years earlier. Lillee dug the ball in all right, as John had divined, but it was the one he aimed at the rib-cage, and as John ducked it caught him amidships. Unlike the Pollock incident, when he felt that he might have carried on, he was in such pain he was forced to retire.

Amiss was soon caught behind off Lillee, Fletcher was caught in the slips off Thomson, and Knott and Titmus both fell to Mallett. Thus at three o'clock, with four wickets to fall and a six o'clock finish, England's caretaker captain came out to resume his innings.

166

He was still in considerable pain. But he did not know that Lillee's bull's-eye had cracked two of his ribs.

At the other end Tony Greig, who had just reached his fifty, swung recklessly at Thomson and was caught in the slips. That was 158 for seven, with the best part of three hours, less the tea interval, still to go.

Somehow the game had to be saved; to come out of it with the Ashes lost, in what might be his only Test Match as captain, was unthinkable for John. And after some useful resistance from Underwood, Willis held out for 98 minutes.

There were fifteen overs to go when Arnold walked to the crease. He held out for eight of them. Then, with only 35 balls left, he was caught off Mallett, and the Ashes changed hands. England thus lost a match they should surely have saved, which they almost certainly would have saved had their confidence not been undermined already. 'Edrich,' wrote Woodcock, 'brought to these last three hours the brand of resolution which would have saved the game had everyone showed it.' The example he set deserved a better reward.

England lost the fifth Test – without John – by 163 runs. The final Test, with Thomson absent and Lillee crocked after bowling six overs, hardly seemed to count. Denness made 188 and Fletcher 146; but once again it was John, after Amiss had been lbw to Lillee for 4, who led the original recovery. His 70 ensured that, despite the imbalance of the run-getting in the final Test, he topped the England averages. That, in a series in which he was the only specialist batsmen whose reputation at the end of it was not left in shreds, was no more than his due.

Four bouncers in an over; that was the ration allowed Jeff Thomson at one point in this series. Three in an over from Lillee. At their speed, a speed equalled by few bowlers in the history of cricket, on wickets of real pace and bounce, such a fusillade, in the opinion of Ray Robinson, was asking too much of human courage. John Edrich, at least, found the resolution to attempt an answer.

After the traumatic events of that winter, it was inevitable

167

that the cry should go up for the disbandment of what was called the old guard. And when John was left out of the Prudential Cup matches, some imagined that he might be one of the discards. Even John himself, after the mental and physical battering he had been exposed to in Australia, might not have minded if he hadn't been called on again.

England clearly had to start yet again to rebuild. But the reluctance of Boycott, the downfall from grace of Amiss, and the absence of alternatives, made the exclusion of John for the moment unthinkable. He was one of only two or three men of that Australia tour party whom England could not possibly do without.

The tragedy of the opening match belonged individually to Denness. After putting the Australians in, and holding them to 186 for 5, he could not halt the recovery that took them to 389. Then, when England batted, disaster overtook them in the shape of a storm, which some said was forecast and others said was not. It turned a good wicket into a treacherous one, soft on top, hard underneath, on which batsmen had little chance. Only one of England's batsmen reached double figures, and that was John with 34, out of England's total of 101. But he failed in the second innings, and this, followed by a first innings failure in the second Test at Lord's, left him somewhat precariously placed when he opened with Barry Wood in the second innings.

Whether or not John would have been swept from the international scene for the last time if he had failed in that innings is an imponderable that only some confessional from the selectors themselves can answer. Nothing was more obvious than that he was out of form and out of touch. He played and missed. When he did connect, he hit the ball straight at the field. But he hung on. And during the innings he found himself.

The whole match was almost unbelievably dramatic. After being 49 for five England reached 315, thanks to Greig (96), Knott (69), and Steele (50); and Australia made an even more amazing recovery to reach 268 (Edwards 99, Lillee 73 not out) after being 81 for seven. Yet the pitch was not to blame, and indeed in the second innings Lillee and Thomson were mastered. John's 175, a feat of massive concentration, provided the backbone, and England were able to declare at 436 for seven; but Australia, with some help from the weather, played out time.

At Headingley the Australians introduced the left-arm fast-medium of Gary Gilmour, the man who had bowled England out in the Prudential Cup; and the overcast conditions were exactly to his liking. This time, however, after getting Wood cheaply, he was met by determined resistance from John (62), who went in first throughout the series, and England's new No. 3 David Steele. These two apart, only Greig made runs, and England's 288 looked vulnerable until Australia collapsed to the slow-left-arm of Edmonds. England made 291 at the second attempt (Steele 92, Greig 49, John 35, Knott 31), and the match was beautifully poised for the last day when the 'Free George Davis' campaigners intruded.

Having lost one Test, England had nothing to show for the advantage they had gained in the other two, and in this four-Test series they could not now regain the Ashes. It did not seem, when Australia made 532 at the Oval and England were dismissed for 191 and were obliged to follow on, that any injustice had been done, unless it was to George Davis; but then came the fight-back. 'Edrich, the old soldier, got the resistance going,' said *The Cricketer,* and he got within four runs of an eighth century against Australia before he was bowled by Lillee. Having started their second innings 341 behind, England were then 209 for three, and Roope and Woolmer completed the recovery.

The recrudescence of John Edrich as England's premier batsman at the age of thirty-eight was as charged with romance as the denouement of any story of fiction. First he had survived the holocaust of fast bowling that had broken the nerve of men whose natural gifts were quite possibly superior to his. Then at Edgbaston, in the first Test of 1975, with his mind and reflexes still stunned by the assault of the previous winter, he had managed to call up something from deep within his resources so that he didn't let England down.

Finally, in that second innings at Lord's, something had happened which had given him renewal. Some inner compulsion had taken hold of him as he struggled to find his form, something which impelled him to bat on and on, exhausting his erstwhile tormentors in a mammoth effort of application that brought him his highest score against Australia.

He had seemed to bat that day in a kind of vacuum, isolated and dispassionate. But the effect had been to rekindle all the ambition he had ever felt for cricket at the top.

There was no sign of staleness in his batting when he led the fight back from what seemed certain defeat at the Oval in September. For him, that series could have lasted for ever.

Epilogue

The switchbacks and vicissitudes of the cricketing Edriches have left their final status in the annals of the game open to controversy – an element to which none of them is unfamiliar. The late arrival and early departure of the ebullient Eric was regretted by all cricket watchers; he brought that special sort of chuckle to the county game which only the really original characters can inspire. Brian, too, typified an element that has always graced the fringes of cricket history – the talented allrounder who has his moments and who makes up in enthusiasm, cheerfulness and team spirit for the gifts which never quite come to fruition. And then there is Geoffrey, whose career strikes the most human note of all. Starting late, like Eric, he showed such dedicated professionalism that he earned a high place amongst post-war Lancashire batsmen, ranking alongside such men as Winston Place, John Ikin and Geoff Pullar, and more recently, David Lloyd, Barry Wood and Harry Pilling. As for his fielding, his 333 catches, in a career spanning only twelve seasons (339 matches), speaks for itself. 'If he'd been around now,' said Eric recently, 'he'd have played for England. He was much the same type of player as David Steele.'

Like his brothers, Bill lost six of his best years to the war. He missed further seasons qualifying for Middlesex, and his three-year banishment from international cricket made further inroads. For those who never saw him at his peak, it may be that his true stature has been somewhat eroded by the continual coupling of his name with Denis Compton. One would not argue that he approached Compton's genius, which was unique; but in his own way he was just as formidable an opponent. No one watched the ball more closely, he had a magnificent defence, and he played all the shots. That shrewd judge Trevor Bailey rates him as a great player who would have been an automatic choice for a world eleven at his peak.

Lastly, John. In 1975 he scored his seventh century against Australia, putting him level with Maurice Leyland as England's greatest left-hander. By being bowled for 96 by Dennis Lillee in the final Test at the Oval he narrowly missed eclipsing Leyland and equalling the record of Herbert Sutcliffe, to whose temperament, perhaps, his is more nearly related. Apart from Sutcliffe, only Hammond (9) and Hobbs (12) have scored more centuries against Australia. Yet that square, strong-armed, unruffled but pugnacious figure will be remembered long after the records have been absorbed into history. He is predictable, and he is unpredictable. He is rocklike, and he is fallible. He is just as likely to get a hundred either way.

For forty years an Edrich has been almost continually in contention for a place in the England team. But from the four Edriches who were playing first-class cricket in 1947, the clan now depends on a single representative. And he, despite all the evidence to the contrary, cannot last for ever. Where is the next generation of Edriches to come from?

At the end of that 1947 season, the idea of a family match was revived, and Bill skippered an Edrich XI that included his three brothers, three of his cousins, three of his uncles, and his father. As succeeding generations have matured they have joined at an early age in what has become almost an annual event. Some of them have developed into cricketers of minor counties standard, but apart from John none has made the first-class game his career. If, as one must surely hope, the name of Edrich is not to revert to the comparative obscurity of village cricket, the family match, generally played today on the beautiful tree-lined ground at Ingham in Norfolk, will be the chrysalis. But either way, it has been a glorious innings.

Career Statistics

Compiled by Irving Rosenwater

WILLIAM JOHN EDRICH

Second son of W. A. Edrich

Born: Lingwood, Norfolk, March 26, 1916.

First-class debut: Minor Counties *v.* Oxford University, Oxford, 1934.

Debut for Middlesex: *v.* Northants, Lord's, 1937.

Middlesex cap: 1937.

Test debut: England *v.* Australia, Trent Bridge, 1938.